Approaching Life With Confidence

Defeat Depression and Anxiety by Taking Charge of Your Mind

Brian K. Chandler
Psy.D.

Approaching Life With Confidence: Defeat
Depression and Anxiety by Taking Charge of Your
Mind

Follow Dr. Chandler at *mypracticalpsychologist.com.*

Cover photo: Haley K. Chandler

Edited by WordEthic, LLC. Visit www.wordethic.com.

WordEthic

YOU'RE ONLY AS GOOD AS YOUR WORDS

With Gratitude

I express my love and appreciation for my wife, Susan, and our four children, Craig, Courtney, Alyssa, and Hayley, who have loved and supported me with all my career aspirations. They have always been my biggest fans and are the driving force for me in doing what I do.

Table of Contents

Follow Dr. Chandler at *mypracticalpsychologist.com*.

By Way Of Introduction

Early in my pursuit of a bachelor's degree, I really wanted to help people be happy. I wanted to learn all about psychology so I could understand what made them tick. I believed I could treat and cure anybody. As I continued my studies in graduate school, I learned many things that I put into practice in clinical settings, moving me toward my goal.

Having worked with children, adolescents, and adults for more than 25 years in the field of mental health, I have observed a myriad of challenges and countless difficult circumstances people face. I have worked with tens of thousands of patients and conducted full psychology batteries on some 8,000 individuals ranging from 3 to 75 years old. I have studied human development, personality theory, psychopathology physiology, and neuropsychology among many other related topics on the human organism.

With all my education and experience, though, I have realized that we don't have all the answers to the problems people face, and what helps them heal is quite varied. What helps one person may be of no benefit to another. To make it worse, any one person's ability to heal can change from day to day.

I often tell patients that we don't know all the variables that contributed to them becoming depressed or anxious or unhappy. We can't simply do a blood test that tells us they are 30 percent depressed, for example, and then prescribe a certain medication to fix the imbalance. Physiology plays a role in emotional health but we never know exactly how much of a part.

This nature vs. nurture debate has endured for decades, perhaps centuries, and still has not been resolved. I believe, as do most professionals in the field of mental health, that nature and nurture both play key roles in individual development. Our nature, our individual genetic makeup, is outside of our ability to control. On the other hand, and this is where this book comes into play, everyone has the ability to make choices about how they think and about how they want to act. That ability varies by the nature and severity of our condition, but we all have the capability and can improve over time. In our daily choices and actions, we find the key to addressing effectively many of the emotional challenges so many people deal with every day.

Some people spend time and energy trying to figure out things that we may never really understand. Theories of psychology are as varied as are treatment approaches. Many clinicians and patients believe they must spend years in intensive psychotherapy to finally figure out the origin of an emotional illness and then spend years reshaping the patient's personality.

There can be benefits to understanding different theories of psychology and implementing various techniques that may help with different aspects of mental illness in certain individuals, but the regular application of the basic principles taught here can help most people avoid or defeat depression and anxiety, improve interpersonal relationships, and lead to much greater happiness in life. The bulk of this improvement stems back to how we decide to think and the behaviors we choose.

That is the purpose of this book, to help you understand and then apply simple principles of human behavior which, if practiced regularly over time, can significantly improve your life.

I hope that makes you happy.

You Can Change Your Life, This Book Can Help

This is a friendly, hands-on book that is meant to help you change. The information can empower you and enable you to achieve greater satisfaction and fulfillment in your life.

It takes your time and best effort to learn and apply these principles, but you will have the tools and guidance you need along the way.

Here is how it is organized:

Decide Now To Start Or To Stop

The first two chapters are designed to help you realize that you can make a significant difference today by starting to do something you should, or to stop doing something you shouldn't. You will have greater determination to take action.

What You See Is What You Are: How Perception Creates Reality

The next section delves into perception from different angles. Perception, how we choose to see life around us, is the primary theme of the book. If you can lay a firm foundation by better understanding your perceptions then you are on your way to changing how you think and how you act.

Selfie-Perception

The third section focuses specifically on self-perception—*you*—as a critical component of your emotional well-being. With this piece in place, you can begin to fully apply what you learn about perceptions to springboard you into interacting more effectively with your world.

You Are In Charge

The fourth section deals with your interactions with the world and how to take control of your environment by learning to behave in ways that promote emotional health and successful relationships. It's pretty cool.

Now, Make It Happen

The final section concludes with some general principles to apply that will help you to have increased gratitude and to understand the root of happiness. Simple practices are encouraged and the element of time is discussed as a final bookend to create a greater awareness of how you can help yourself by managing time wisely.

Let's begin....

Section 1—Decide Now To Start Or To Stop

Your Best Day Is Today

You Pick Up Both Ends Of The Stick

Your Best Day Is Today

If I told you today could be one of the best days of the rest of your life, what would you think? When I suggest this to patients, some ask if I am giving them a million dollars. Some teenagers at the hospital where I work shout, "I'm getting discharged!" Some want to meet a celebrity while others want super powers.

I don't have a million dollars, I can't arrange to meet a celebrity, nor can I bestow super powers on anyone. However, I can promise that as you understand and apply what is in this chapter, this truly can be one of the best days of your life. It has nothing to do with me giving you anything or doing something for you. Rather, it has everything to do with you and your choices, and your answer to this question:

Is there something, big or small, that you could do today that would change the course of your life?

Perhaps it's something you could start doing or something you could stop doing that would have a significant impact, but all of us have those same options to change our lives, every day, something to do or to stop doing.

Let's look at some examples.

Drug and alcohol addictions are extremely debilitating and can ruin lives. We all know someone who is addicted to drugs or alcohol and have seen what it does to them and those around them. It is likely that you also know someone who has quit using drugs or alcohol and have seen the positive impact that has on their life. At some point, those who quit using the addictive substance had to *decide* they were done with it, regardless of how many rehab programs they completed. You may have watched someone go through rehab many times only to fall off the wagon and find themselves right back where they were. Until someone decides they are done, finally done, they can go to a hundred rehab programs and it simply will not last. It's their decision to quit that ultimately enables them to exert the will power and access the resources to ensure that they stop and never go back.

It is the same for each of us, for me and for you. If you are addicted to a substance today, you can make a choice to stop using that substance today and it will change the course of your life.

9

How about a person struggling with weight? He could decide that today he is going to change his habits by eating more nutritious food and not overeating. Today he is going to start exercising. I'm not suggesting this is easy, nor am I suggesting that someone who is obese is going to become physically fit in a short time, or any time for that matter. All I suggest is that if someone who has struggled with weight for many years decides today to make those simple choices, it will change the rest of his life. Even if he does not become thin or even average by medical standards, he will certainly become healthier and add months or years to his life with much less likelihood of physical and emotional problems.

Let's consider some other things that people can do today that could change the course of their lives.

I knew a young woman who did not like herself and did not respect herself. She decided one day, after being taught this principle, that she was not going to disrespect herself any longer and she would look for good things about herself. What do you think her life is like now? What is she doing differently and how is the world responding to her now? How are her relationships improved, her level of confidence, her life satisfaction?

One person may simply choose to smile and make eye contact with others. Think of the difference this could make in someone's life. If he had previously been shy and introverted without many friends, what do you think would happen as he made this change? Surely more people would smile back and even say hello. He would have more opportunities to talk with people and consequently make more friends. As people smiled at him and talked with him and became his friend, he would certainly feel better about himself and his self-esteem would increase dramatically.

Again, the thing that you could choose to do or choose to stop doing does not have to be a big thing. The key is that you start today and be consistent. Let time be your ally.

Time is your ally because new habits take time. You may stumble on your new path. You may doubt your ability to change. You may think, "that's just the way I am," but it's really just the way you were yesterday. The way you are today is still being determined. Don't give up but pick yourself up. Take that next step, keep going, and keep picking yourself up. Each day is new, with a new you.

Perhaps an orienteering analogy can illustrate how starting or stopping something small today can have a huge impact on life in years to come. You need a compass for orienteering, and on a compass there are 360 degrees. That's a lot of degrees in just a small circle. Think of how small one degree is on that compass. Tiny. Despite being so small, over a significant distance it has a big impact. If you were navigating a course seeking treasure and you were one degree off over the course of one mile you would miss your treasure by 92 feet. That is just one degree and one mile. Imagine how far off you would be if it was two or three degrees and if it was two or three or five or ten miles. A simple change today can have a huge impact on your life, good or bad, positive or negative, one week or one year or five years or ten years down the road.

We often become discouraged, feeling we have not been productive or have missed out on chances to do things when we were younger. We may look at old friends whom we perceive to be much more successful than we are and feel that we are a failure. Consider this Chinese proverb:

> The best time to plant a tree was 20 years ago. The second best time is now.

We can choose to make a change and start today because, before we know it, next year will come, and then the year after. Pretty soon, it will be several years down the road and we could have done lots of different things that would have put us in a much different place.

Let me share a few examples of people who struggled early in life only to become hugely successful because they decided to keep on trying.

Harland Sanders was fired from several jobs before finally starting his own restaurant. This also failed and he found himself out of business and broke at age 65. However, he kept trying and eventually patented and trademarked his "finger lickin' good" recipe. The Colonel sold the company for millions at age 73 but continued on as the well-paid symbol for KFC.

Ray Kroc worked as a salesman hawking milkshake devices until 1954 when he was 52 years old. He became a franchising agent for McDonald's, then president of the corporation, and bought the company in 1961, growing it into the world's largest fast food franchise.

Samuel L. Jackson is a famous movie star but he had only small roles before landing an award-winning part in Spike Lee's film *Jungle Fever* at age 43.

J. K. Rowling, author of the *Harry Potter* series, was a divorced, single mother dependent on government welfare. She conceived the idea for the Harry Potter story in 1990 when she was 25 years old. After the initial idea and before publishing the first book in 1997, she lost her mother, had her first child, divorced her first husband, and endured relative poverty. Her book was rejected by several publishers before finally being given a chance.

One of the most famous Americans had a string of failures and significant life challenges before he finally reached the highest office in the land. I have a plaque in my office with a picture of Abraham Lincoln that lists a series of failures and tragedies before his final great success. It reads:

1831   failed in business;

1832   ran for state legislature and lost;

1832   lost job and wanted to go to law school but couldn't get in;

1833   borrowed money from a friend to begin a business but by the end of the year was bankrupt;

1834   ran for state legislature again but this time won;

1835   was engaged to be married but fiancée died;

1836   had a total nervous breakdown and was in bed for six months;

1838   sought to become speaker of the state legislature and was defeated;

1840   sought to become elector and was defeated;

1843   ran for Congress and lost;

1846   ran again for Congress and this time he won;

1848   ran for reelection to Congress but lost;

1849   sought job of land officer in home state but was rejected;

1854   ran for U. S. Senate and lost;

1856   sought vice presidential nomination at party's national convention and received less than 100 votes;

1858   ran for U. S. Senate again and lost;

1860   elected as 16th President of the United States of America.

These people and countless more kept moving forward. They faced adversity and temporary failure but continued to try. They picked themselves up and kept going. They never stopped believing that one choice today can change everything.

For you, even a small change today can change the course of your life. So let me ask again: what can you choose to do or to stop doing today that will make today one of the best days of the rest of your life? What small but significant course correction can you make today? There are lots of options, but perhaps there is one thing that jumps out right away and you thought about it even as you read the paragraphs above.

I challenge you to give it a try and see what you can do. Today.

You Pick Up Both Ends Of The Stick

I conduct psychological evaluations on a variety of individuals for a host of reasons. In a fairly typical scenario, a 26-year-old mother named Rhonda is sent to my office by Division of Family Services (DFS) because her three children, all from different fathers, are in state custody as a result of a hotline call by a neighbor. During the home investigation, the DFS worker discovers a dilapidated mobile home with unsanitary living conditions. Rhonda's boyfriend is a drug addict and is physically abusive to her and her children. The family has no money because neither the woman nor her boyfriend has a job and none of the fathers pay child support. Rhonda is sent to me to determine if she can become a competent parent and eventually have her children returned to her.

The life principle I want to emphasize has to do with understanding how the choices we make in one part of our life can and will impact other parts of our life. It's all about behaviors and consequences. If we pick up one end of a stick we pick up the other end, too. If we choose a behavior we also choose the consequence attached to that behavior.

I see more and more people who live irresponsibly. They choose a certain behavior but think they can somehow avoid any consequences. They want to drink and drive and they are surprised when they get a DUI or have an accident. They want to have unprotected sex and are surprised when they have an unwanted pregnancy. They want to drop out of school and are surprised when they have difficulty landing a good job.

Obviously, the situation in which Rhonda finds herself is extremely undesirable. I ask myself at what point did she say, "Someday in my mid-twenties, I want to have three kids from three different fathers, none of whom are involved in their lives or paying child support; I want a deadbeat drug addict for a boyfriend who is abusive to me and my children; I want to live in a dilapidated mobile home with unsanitary living conditions and have no education or job skills and no money to support myself and my children."

Rhonda never once said this or even thought this. She'd have to be crazy to say that. So how did it happen? What went wrong? Is she simply a victim of bad luck? No, she is not. I'm sure you can figure out what happened. Let's go back a few years and look at some of her choices that she certainly felt would not have long-term ill effects in her life.

About age 13, Rhonda decided to experiment with marijuana. She began using fairly regularly and it became a habit. By age 14, she found herself at parties where a lot of other drugs and alcohol were available. She thought, "Everyone does this. I'm just a kid having a little fun." When she started high school she had become quite a partier and now, because of her associations, made connections with even more partiers and got fairly deep into the drug scene.

As is often the case, when using drugs and partying, people make poor choices about relationships and sex. In addition to using a multitude of drugs, Rhonda began to have sex with multiple partners and much of the sex was unprotected. This resulted in pregnancy at age 15 and a baby at age 16. She was a sophomore in high school when she became pregnant, which made it difficult to attend class consistently. She already had started a pattern of missing school because hanging out with her druggie friends was more fun than going to boring old school all day. So when the due date drew closer, even though the school district had a special program for pregnant students, Rhonda chose to drop out.

You can see how the paths she chose early in her life led to misery and heartache as a 26-year-old. She continued to use drugs throughout her teens and into her early adulthood. All of her kids' fathers were associations she made while using drugs and, no surprise, they have chosen to have nothing to do with their children. Having dropped out of school, Rhonda had little opportunity to secure gainful employment and struggled to make ends meet.

When did Rhonda decide to be in the situation she is in, having her kids taken away, and needing an evaluation in my office? She decided at ages 13 and 14 and 16 when she chose to use drugs, to have unprotected sex, and to drop out of school. We can choose behaviors every day in our life but once we have chosen the behavior we automatically get the consequence with it. We may not fear or even see the consequence because it seems far away, but it is there, waiting, and there is no escaping it.

Let's look at another example of making choices early in life that can have profound effects years later. Until recently, most people had never heard of Ben Carson. Ben is known because of his candidacy for the Republican Party's 2016 presidential nomination and as the current U. S. Secretary of Housing and Urban Development. You may know he is a retired neurosurgeon but you may not know about his early years.

Ben was born in Detroit to a single, teen mother. His mother was one of more than 20 children and had a rough life. She had Ben and another son and was trying to raise them herself. When Ben was in fifth grade, he was at the bottom of his class academically. One day the teacher gave a 20-point quiz and after the students finished, she told them to give their paper to the student beside them to grade. Once graded, the papers were returned to the students. The teacher asked the students to call out their test scores to see how each of them had done. After Ben had called out his test score, the teacher, knowing Ben was the dumbest kid in her class, said, "Wow, Ben, a nine; that's good." Nine out of 20 for Ben was a big improvement, but, unfortunately, she had misunderstood what Ben said. The boy next to Ben who had scored his test yelled out to the teacher, "He didn't say nine, he said none."

Ben's mother was determined to make a better life for her boys. She worked cleaning homes to make ends meet. One day as she worked she realized something. The people for whom she cleaned houses had something she and her boys didn't have: libraries. They read books. When she returned home that day she made a decision to change things. She gathered her boys around and said to Ben and his brother, "We are going to make some changes in our home. From now on you are going to watch just three TV programs a week and the rest of the time you are going to read books. We are going to the library and you are going to check out books and write me two reports a week."

You can imagine how two young boys responded to a directive like that. Limiting TV time and requiring two book reports every week? As much as Ben and his brother resisted, their mother was firm in her resolve to make a change. They proceeded to do what their mother directed. Ben, who was at the bottom of his class in the fifth grade, by the seventh grade was at the top of his class. Ben went on to graduate from high school and attended Yale University on a scholarship. He graduated from Yale and went to John's Hopkins University Medical School and by age 34 became the Head of Pediatric Neurosurgery at that school. He was the surgeon who led a team of doctors who successfully separated Siamese twins joined at the head.

The choices we make are often not earth-shattering but are simple things done consistently which, over time, can make a big difference. Bronco Mendenhall, who is the head football coach at the University of

Virginia and has coached college football for 27 years, spoke of this life principle as he observed very successful football players over many years. He stated that All-Pro football players are not necessarily more talented than other football professionals. The difference is that All-Pro players do the little things longer, better, and more often than other football players.

What choices have you made today? Where are they leading you? What are the consequences of those choices? Are you choosing responsibly or are you living in the moment?

Section 2—What You See Is What You Are: How Perception Creates Reality

Things Are Not Always As They Appear

Jump Into The Loop: Why Your Frame Of Reference Makes It Okay

Paradigms: Way More Than 20 Cents

Confirmatory Hypothesis Testing: Is Eddie As Dumb As He Thinks?

Think Outside The Box

Mediating Variables And Other Challenges

Things Are Not Always As They Appear

It is human nature for us to make judgments. In fact, it is good and necessary for us to do so, but it is not always easy to judge correctly.

As mentioned earlier, our judgments have consequences, some more serious than others. Some are trivial, like which brand of raisin bran to have for breakfast, but many can cause us to be unnecessarily burdened or to miss out on some of life's good things.

Let me illustrate this idea with a couple of optical illusions.

These figures may be familiar to you but they still make a valid point.

Take a look and see what you think.

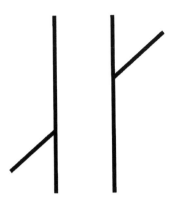

Figure 1

Are the diagonal lines on each side of the vertical lines part of the same line but with the middle cut out? If you connected the diagonal lines together, would they make a straight line or would it be three segments of a crooked line?

It doesn't look like one straight line, so it must be crooked, right? Get out your ruler and check it.

Are the two horizontal lines below equal in length? Does the top one look shorter than the bottom one? That's how it appears, doesn't it? Again, get out your ruler and measure them.

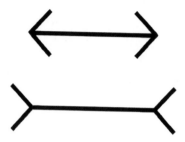

Figure 2

Of course, they are the same length, despite what we think we see. Things are not always as they appear.

Think of other things in life that are not always as they appear. Most of us have a good friend we didn't like when we first met. Perhaps we thought they were obnoxious and we would never believe we could become friends, or in some cases, marry the other person. How do we misjudge someone so much at first? How does that happen?

It happens all the time because we are human and humans often make judgments based on very little data. We mistakenly believe that the tiny bit of information we've gathered gives us a complete picture when, in fact, it is such a small sample of what is really there. If the circle in Figure 3 represents a person, the dot inside the circle represents the facts we have and, ultimately, determines what we think of the person. This is clearly narrow-minded, not to mention unfair and unwise, yet we do it all the time.

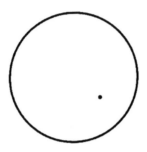

Figure 3

My favorite example of making judgments based on too little information comes from a Stephen Covey book I read long ago. The story is about a man on a subway:

> When the train stops, several people board, including a man with three young children. The father sits in front of the man who tells the story. The three children never take a seat, but mess around in the aisle and fight each other.

As the subway continues, these unruly children bump into passengers, step on toes, and become increasingly aggravating. The man becomes impatient with the father who obviously cannot manage his kids and is clearly not a good parent.

After a couple more minutes, the man taps the father on the shoulder to confront him. The father looks dazed as the man expresses annoyance and asks him to get his children under control. The father haltingly replies in a somber voice, "We just came from the hospital where my wife died; I guess they don't know how to handle it."

Of course, this is not what the man expected to hear, and he offers a sincere apology. The man feels terrible. The kids are still fighting and being obnoxious, but is the man still annoyed? No, of course not. Nothing has changed in this situation, except, that is, the new information. Because of this, he now *sees* his world in a totally different way and, consequently, *feels* very differently. Suddenly, he has an increased measure of tolerance for these young children. He no longer is mad at them or their father but only feels compassion, and would even like to help them if he could.

Remember, things are not always as they appear.

You can see the wisdom in gathering more information before we become too rigid in our judgments. Judging too soon with insufficient information can cause us to be burdened with feelings of irritability or hostility towards another person.

Let's consider another example. Allow me to create a scenario that will illustrate this point well. As you're driving along, a man pulls out of a side street and cuts you off. Are you mad? I bet you are if you're like me. This surely has happened to every driver. Let's see how this plays out. You decide to tailgate this moron and see where he's going in such a hurry. After a mile, he approaches the local hospital. He hurriedly turns toward the Emergency Room entrance. As you slow down, you see him stop his car, jump out, run to the passenger side and scoop up a little child then run inside. How do you feel now? Are you still mad at this man? Is he still that jerk who doesn't know how to drive and shouldn't have a license? Of course not. You now have a little more information and, as a result, you can make a much more informed judgment and, consequently, feel very differently. Instead of anger, you feel compassion for this man and the little child.

After 20 years working at a psychiatric hospital, I have had countless experiences of seeing patients as they are admitted and making a cursory judgment about them. They usually look haggard and very unhappy to be there. Often they are hostile and uncooperative. This type of belligerence often continues for a day or two and frequently creates great difficulty for me in completing the necessary psychological tests because they simply refuse to engage with me.

I specifically remember a 14-year-old female who was antagonistic with staff and other patients on the unit, and who refused to participate in any activities. I went into her room to test the waters and my luck at trying to administer some tests. The first time she was hostile and refused. The second time, a day later, yielded the same result. On the third attempt the following day, she actually sat up in her bed, made eye contact with me, and engaged in a pleasant conversation. After a little small talk leading into a few clinical questions, she agreed to allow me to administer some tests. As I came to know her and as she started attending my therapy groups each day, I saw her in a whole different light.

Research has shown that first impressions are powerful to humans as we create cognitive files for a person, place, or situation. Part of the problem is, once we have the initial file, we think we know the person and often never seek to gather more information that may lead us to modify our file. These first impressions provide the bulk of the material used to open these cognitive files and we often have a hard time modifying them.

How many files do you have that need modification? How many circles with a little dot do you have stored away in your brain? Most of us, I dare say, have hundreds of them. Which ones are you going to modify by gathering more information so you will have a greater understanding of a person and a new perspective that can help you feel very differently?

Pick one and get to work. Your new best friend could be waiting for you.

Jump Into The Loop: Why Your Frame Of Reference Makes It Okay

Our frame of reference is vitally important because it directs how we see ourselves, others, and everything in the world. There is no way *not* to have a frame of reference. The question is: what is your frame of reference and how is it serving you? Look at Figure 4 and tell me what you see.

Figure 4

It seems simple enough, right? I bet you see the word p-o-o-l. Is that right? Do you see anything else? What else could it be? Do you see the word l-o-o-p? How about p-o-l-o? Is that all it is? Is it just letters and words? Could it be anything else?

Okay, we're stuck with four letters, which is all fine and good if you speak English, but what if you're not a native English speaker? Let's say you're from China. What would you see? You wouldn't recognize the word p-o-o-l because you don't even know the word exists. To you, it is just some English writing.

Now, look at the object in Figure 5.

Figure 5

What do you see? To an English speaker, it is some lines that seem to make a crude design. To a person from China, it is easily recognized as the character for mountain, pronounced shan.

Look back at Figure 4. If you are a mathematician, you might see numbers, maybe some zeros, maybe the number 100, maybe a 9, if you really use your imagination. What if you are a musician? Would you see music notes, maybe whole notes and perhaps a quarter note? What if you were two years old? You probably would just see circles and lines. Someone who is fond of theater or opera may see opera glasses. We could go on and on, couldn't we?

What we see has much less to do with what is on the page and far more to do with what is in our heads. So to apply this to life, what we see in the world often has less to do with what's out there and much more to do with what is in our heads. As with the word p-o-o-l, your background would determine what you pictured in your mind after you read or saw the word. A swimmer would read p-o-o-l and form an image of a swimming pool. A billiards player, on the other hand, would likely picture a pool table.

An unattributed plaque in my office reads, "We see the world, not as it is, but as we are." This is a peculiar statement. What does it mean? Again, what we see in the world every day has little to do with what is out there and has so much to do with what is in our head. In fact, two people in the same situation could have a very different perspective and ultimately a very different experience. The life principle that I like to teach is this: two people can look at the same thing and see something different.

Let's look at a couple more examples.

When my children were little, they liked me to read the Berenstain Bears books to them. There is one in particular that I remember quite well, *The Berenstain Bears Learn About Strangers*. Mother and Father Bear are teaching Brother and Sister Bear about strangers. Brother Bear is unfazed by what his parents teach him, but Sister Bear is completely freaked out by the thought of strangers. She clearly expects some stranger to come along any day and snatch her up and hurt her. In the middle of the book, as you open up the page, it is split in two with a top and bottom. Both show the village green, but they look quite different. On the top part of the page, the sun is shining, the animals are playing, bunnies, raccoons, and butterflies smiling, other bears having fun together, just a wonderful summer day. The bottom half of the page is dark and gloomy. The animals look mean and the other bears menacing, some wearing trench coats with shifty, devious stares. Once again, it was the exact same village green, but it looked so different to Brother Bear compared to Sister Bear, not because of what was out there, but because of what was in their heads.

Here is another example with dogs. At the hospital where I do a lot of my work with children and adolescents, the recreation therapists would often bring therapy dogs around so the patients could interact with them. They would ask if they could come into the group for a few minutes and let the kids pet the dog.

Most of the time, the kids were happy to have the dog come in. However, there have been a handful of patients over the years who were not eager to see the dog. In fact, some were down right afraid. Why? Maybe that's too obvious but it is exactly what we are talking about. The few kids who were fearful had a bad experience with dogs in their past and therefore were afraid of the dog. To them, the dog was an animal that could bite them. To the rest of the group, most of whom had dogs as pets and loved playing with dogs, the therapy dog was a wonderful, playful diversion from the arduous task of therapy.

There is an optical illusion that teaches this principle well, from the same book by Steven Covey I read years ago. I have adapted it to better address this principle.

I call your attention to Figure 6.

Figure 6

After you have noted what you see, take a look at Figure 7.

What do you see? Most people see a young lady. Can you see the same young lady in Figure 7 that you saw in Figure 6?

It's really the same lady but the sketch is more refined.

Figure 7

Now I will give you another sketch of a woman in Figure 8.

Take a few seconds to save this image in your mind. Now, look back at Figure 7. Do you see the young lady you saw before or do you see something different? Perhaps you see an old lady? Or do you see a young lady and an old lady depending on how you look at it?

I have done this exercise in thousands of therapy groups over the years and have learned an important principle. I give the rough sketch of the young woman

Figure 8

to half of the group and the rough sketch of the old woman to the other half of the group.

After they view it for a minute, I take it from them. Then I give everyone a copy of the more refined sketch where you can see the young woman and the old woman, depending on how you look at it. I then ask group members what they see. Inevitably, the ones who had the rough sketch of the young woman first will see the young woman in the more refined picture, and the ones who had the rough sketch of the old woman first will see the old woman.

I have them turn their pictures around to allow everyone to see that they all have the same picture. As they argue back and forth and start showing each other how it looks like a young woman or an old woman, the group members begin to see both women in their picture.

This exercise simulates real life in that we learn, or are conditioned, to see things certain ways by our upbringing, culture, worldview and, essentially, by all of our life experiences. What we see is simply *what we see* and someone else inevitably sees it a little bit differently.

We have problems in many of our relationships because we think the way we see something is *the right way* or *the only way* and the other person's way of seeing must, therefore, be wrong. Convinced we are right, we try to force others to see it our way. When they don't, we become upset and often argue and draw judgments about these people who are strange because they just don't see things the right way.

Chances are you can think of a person with whom you've experienced a difference of opinion. Apply what you've read in this chapter to your relationship with him or her. Can you see how they may see something differently than you? Consider apologizing to this person if there was a disagreement and be willing to stay more open-minded in the future.

Paradigms: Way More Than 20 Cents

The unique quality of a paradigm is that we typically don't even know it's there, yet it dictates the way we see things and how we operate in most aspects of our lives. A paradigm is a way of thinking or a point of view. The best way to discuss paradigms is to give examples to illustrate paradigms in history as well as in our current daily life.

Most of us have heard of Christopher Columbus, who is generally credited with discovering America, but few of us have heard of a *geography paradigm*. Columbus had a different view of the world than most people. He wanted to charter ships and prove that he could sail around the world. Do you remember what most people thought in the 1490s? They thought he was crazy because, as everyone knew, as was obvious, the world was flat. Columbus would be killed because after sailing a certain distance he would get to the edge of the earth and fall off.

The *geography paradigm* of the day was that the world was flat. If you would have asked people about their geography paradigm, they would have been confused, and probably a little suspicious. Had you replied that they had a geography paradigm that the world was flat, they would have said, "Paradigm, smaradigm. It's a well-known fact that the world is flat and that idiot, Columbus, is going to get himself killed sailing off the edge of the earth." They didn't realize they had a paradigm related to the geography of the world. To them, it was simply a fact, the obvious truth.

That is the first principle of paradigms. We typically don't even recognize they are there. We think that is just the way it is. The way I perceive the world, a particular situation, is just the way it is. I'm not putting any cognition into this equation. That's just how it is.

The second principle about paradigms is that they often are extremely limiting because we think and behave in ways consistent with the paradigm. Consequently, we remain limited or stuck in a certain perception that doesn't allow us to move outside the safety of our paradigm. In 1492, most people remained very limited in their view of the world. As a result, those people did not venture out very far into the ocean and, therefore, never came to discover new lands or trade partners.

Let's consider a more contemporary paradigm from the public schools. If asked, my 17-year-old daughter would respond, without hesitation, that American students must complete 12 grades before they can graduate from high school. "Everyone knows that," she would say. If pressed to explain why, why not 10 grades or 14 grades, she would repeat that students must have 12 grades to graduate. If I asked, "who says," she would roll her eyes the way 17-year-old daughters do and say, "Dad, that's just the way it is. That's what the school decided."

How many grades did you complete to graduate from high school? If you are an American who went to school in the past 70 years, your answer would most likely be 12. But why? Who decided on 12 grades and not 10 or 14? I'm not suggesting 12 is bad or good, I'm simply making clear that in the United States there is an *education paradigm* that says we must complete 12 grades to graduate from high school. When someone like me questions the paradigm, people usually aren't even aware there is a paradigm. They just think I'm weird or am being silly, but I'm really not. I honestly wonder who decided that 12 is the optimum number of grades necessary to finish secondary education.

Remember the two principles of paradigms, that we often don't know they are there and that they often limit us. Chances are that few of you ever questioned why there are 12 grades while growing up. You just took it as absolute truth, simply as the way it is, with no choice in the matter. To demonstrate how our paradigms can limit us, consider this question: "Do all kids need 12 grades to graduate?" Perhaps there are some brighter than average students who would be better served by completing 10 or 11 grades and starting college early. Also, there are students who benefit in the long-term by being held back a grade. To stick rigidly to the *education paradigm* would limit some people and create potential problems for others.

Here is another facet of the *education paradigm*. When I was in grade school, classrooms were rigidly structured with four or five rows of desks with five or six desks in each row, all lined up facing the teacher's desk and the chalkboard. As I visited my kids in their elementary school classes, I noticed their seating arrangements were much different. They were grouped into pods of four students in a square all facing each other. What a crazy idea, right? What happened to the rows of chairs all facing the teacher? Well, I think you're catching on. Sitting in rows was part of the *education paradigm* and probably related to concern over kids talking in class and not paying attention to the teacher. Yet, we have learned kids working together in a cooperative setting often helps them learn better, and the issue of distraction is minimal.

Another aspect of the *education paradigm* of my day was that everyone traveled outside their home to a facility where they had paid educators to teach them lessons. It definitely is different today for some students. Chances are you know someone who is home-schooled, or you were home-schooled yourself. Where we lived back in my childhood, homeschooling was simply staying home and playing hooky. There was no such thing as homeschooling. The paradigm has shifted, hasn't it? Many students are well-served by being schooled at home and, had we stuck to the old paradigm, who knows how these students would have done.

Let's look at a *relationship paradigm* because I believe this is where we face a lot of our problems. A man may have a very strong sense of masculine and feminine expectations or husband and wife roles in a marriage relationship. This man may see himself as the primary breadwinner who works away from home and provides for his family's physical needs. The woman's role is to stay home and take care of the cooking, cleaning, and child rearing.

You can imagine where this paradigm began for the man—with his own upbringing. That's how Dad and Mom did it and it seemed to work, so that must be the only way to do it, right? Wrong! Let's say that his wife grew up in a very different environment where her father was not around and instead, her mother was the primary breadwinner and managed all the household matters, as well. This woman would have learned that women can be quite independent and do not need a man to take care of them. She may feel trapped and want to get a part-time job outside the home. This could breed feelings of ingratitude or incompetence in the husband, feeling his wife thinks he is not an effective provider. He may also be frustrated because, as she is working outside the home, a much larger portion of the child care responsibilities are relegated to him. Consequently, he feels he is doing some of her job and that she should be home managing the children instead of out working.

We could go on and on about paradigms. Henry Ford revolutionized manufacturing by creating the assembly line, challenging the *manufacturing paradigm* of the day. There are other business paradigms, nutrition paradigms, health care paradigms, mental health paradigms and on and on.

What I want to get to now are your *personal paradigms*. Again, applying the first principle of paradigms, you need to closely examine aspects of your life that are not functioning at an optimum level and start to dig deep to see if there are *personal paradigms* of which you are unaware, yet you live by. The second principle relates to being stuck and not able to progress because of your *personal paradigm*. You may think it's your boss, your profession, your community, your spouse, or your relationship that is the problem when actually it is your own way of seeing things—your paradigm.

Perhaps you are only a teacher and think you could never be the principal. Perhaps you are a lower level worker and could never be a supervisor. Perhaps you are an employee and could never be an employer or business owner. Until you shift your paradigm, nothing is going to change, because in your world it can't change. You may think, for example, the only way to make ends meet and get out of debt is to get a raise at your current job, to work harder and show your supervisor that you deserve a raise. That may well be true in your current paradigm.

But consider a paradigm shift. Getting a raise at your current job is not the only way to make ends meet and get out of debt. Perhaps you can work harder and show your supervisor that you deserve to be promoted, and then you become a supervisor. Perhaps you need to change jobs, find a position where you can further develop your talents and where your opportunities and earning potential are much greater.

As you consider fundamental changes in how you look at yourself and at your world, you will be surprised by what might happen.

Confirmatory Hypothesis Testing: Is Eddie As Dumb As He Thinks?

Think back to high school science. Do you remember developing a hypothesis then carrying out an experiment to see if your idea was accurate? Just as scientists have hypotheses, so do we. In fact, we have many hypotheses in all aspects of our lives. We have hypotheses about ourselves, about other people, about politics, about nutrition, and so on.

Here is where yours differs from a scientific hypothesis and why many people have trouble with self-esteem or interpersonal relationships: we don't realize that what we think is often just a hypothesis, not a fact. We believe our hypothesis is the truth, rather than a theory or an educated guess, and we think everyone else sees this way, too.

Here is an example to illustrate.

Let's take Eddie, a 15-year-old male who thinks he is dumb, ugly, and nobody likes him. Do you know any one like Eddie? Walking down a hallway in school one day, a girl walks toward him. As she gets close she turns her head, looks away, and says nothing to him. What does Eddie think? How does he explain her behavior? He will most likely conclude that she didn't even want to look at him, let alone talk to him, because he is dumb and ugly and nobody likes him.

Now, you're an intelligent person. What are some other possible explanations for the girl's behavior? Your list may include some of the following:

The girl is shy.

The girl thinks she is dumb and ugly and nobody likes her.

The girl is busy.

The girl's mind is on a problem with a friend.

The girl is thinking about her next class.

The girl is worried about something at home or at work.

The girl has a boyfriend and is very loyal to him.

The girl was distracted by something on the other side of the hall.

And on and on and on. You probably thought of other possibilities. Young Eddie doesn't even consider these possibilities because he is convinced that he is dumb and ugly and nobody likes him. In fact, he is so committed to his hypothesis that he doesn't even realize that it is just a hypothesis. He thinks it is simply true. If it is *true* then it's easy and sensible to explain the girl's behavior this way.

Let's continue to illustrate how a hypothesis developed over years can stick because we believe it is accurate.

The next day, Eddie walks down another hallway at school and another girl approaches him. She gets closer, closer, closer, until finally, she looks at him, smiles, and says, "Hello." What does Eddie think? "Wow! She likes me." Right? No.

How could he make sense out of this girl's behavior given his hypothesis? I bet you can figure it out. He says to himself, "She's just a really nice person. She says that to everybody." Or maybe he thinks, "She feels sorry for me because I'm so pitiful. She's trying to make me feel good." These thoughts enable him to continue living within his hypothesis.

You get the idea that no matter what happens, Eddie makes it fit his hypothesis. Now, let's really drive it home and show you how Eddie behaves in a manner that almost guarantees his hypothesis will stay stuck.

One day early in the school year, Eddie walks into class a bit slumped over, with his head hanging down, avoiding eye contact. He chooses a seat far from everyone and looks at the floor as he sits down. How do you think other kids in class respond? Probably not favorably, right? How would kids in your school respond? Most likely they would ignore him. Eddie thinks they are ignoring him because, you guessed it, he is dumb and ugly and nobody likes him.

Let's consider other possible responses. A caring person may come and ask if something is wrong. If that happens, what does Eddie think while clinging to his hypothesis? "They clearly see that something is wrong with me."

Other less kind kids might giggle and perhaps make snide remarks or throw wadded up paper at him, which would lead him to feel picked on because he is dumb and ugly and nobody likes him.

Eddie is engaged in what we call behavioral self-confirmation. He behaves the way he sees himself, which in turn leads his world to respond to him that same way, which then serves to reinforce his hypothesis.

53

Let's apply this to another situation, to a student and teacher at Eddie's school. A student named Mike has this hypothesis: Mrs. Smith is strict and mean and she plays favorites with the smart kids. On the first day of school, Mike is chatting with friends in the back of the room when Mrs. Smith calls out for them to please stop talking because class is starting.

What does Mike immediately think? Mrs. Smith is yelling at him because she's strict and mean. Is this true? Maybe, but probably not. Is this the only possible explanation for Mrs. Smith's behavior? Certainly not.

Let's consider some other possible reasons. How about she simply wants to start class and do her job so she's asking the students to stop talking and listen to the teacher who is, after all, in charge. Perhaps she is not feeling well and is a bit irritable. Maybe because it's the start of the school year, like many other teachers, she is trying to establish her authority and is being strict initially, but will lighten up a few weeks into the semester.

There are other plausible explanations for her behavior, but Mike is so stuck on his hypothesis he is not willing to entertain any other explanation. Let's continue and see how Mike's hypothesis is not easily changed.

A couple of days later, he sees Mrs. Smith talking to a student and she appears to be kind and reasonable. What does Mike think? Does he throw out his hypothesis because of this observation of Mrs. Smith? How can he explain her behavior? How about like this: "This kid is smart and a brown-noser so Mrs. Smith is being nice to him because she likes smart brown-nosers." As Mike clings to his hypothesis, his behavior will follow suit. He's unlikely to reach out to Mrs. Smith and be friendly with her but will talk behind her back and be disrespectful. Consequently, how does Mrs. Smith treat Mike? She probably has to get on to him for inappropriate behavior which only confirms his hypothesis.

A principle similar to personal hypotheses has to do with files in our brain. Let me share a personal experience to explain.

Many years ago, as a missionary in Taiwan, I needed to learn Mandarin Chinese. Because the language is made up of characters, the way we learned Chinese was through writing out Chinese words in romanization, a way to convert writing from one system to another. One method to help me learn the language was to write 10 Chinese words on an index card each day and diligently study those words as I was out in public and interacting with people.

After a couple of weeks, I was amazed by what was happening. The very day I would study a list of words I would hear them out on the streets. What a crazy surprise!

A couple of weeks beyond this initial observation, I finally understood what was really happening. When I studied a list of words, I would hear them that day. I mistakenly believed that the day I heard a word was the first time that word had been used in my presence. The words I studied were common, everyday words, and I realized that the words I studied and heard on any given day were used by people the day before; however, the day before I studied them they were not words to me but just noise. The words were always there, they just were not there for me until I had a place for them in my brain. For all intents and purposes, they did not exist in my world because they did not yet exist in my brain. I had no file on them.

So here is the important life principle to learn.

If it doesn't exist in your brain, it doesn't exist in your world.

The converse is also true.

If it does exist in your brain that's all that exists in your world.

So what we see is determined by what we know, and that with which we have experience. We could go so far as to say what we see is determined by what we believe.

Here is another example that perhaps many of us can understand. My wife knows very little about automobiles. The makes and models are essentially meaningless to her. Cars are big or small, to her, red or blue. Beyond that, there is not much else, and she holds little interest in changing.

Let's pretend our neighbor pulls into our driveway with a brand new Honda Accord. She calls to my wife and says, "Hey, come check out my new car." My wife walks over and examines the new Accord. She gets in it with our neighbor and goes for a ride. They return home and my wife goes on with the activities of her day.

Little does she know that she has opened a file in her brain on Honda Accords that she previously did not have. What do you think will happen the next couple of days as she drives around town with this new file in her brain? You guessed it. She will see Honda Accords all over. Were those cars there the day before our neighbor bought her new Accord? Yes, of course, they were, but before my wife had an Accord file they were just a car, small, blue.

Now that my wife has a file in her brain on Honda Accords, her brain will register them as she sees them because this new file has opened up her mind and helped her see the world a little differently.

Terry Seamons, current BYU Alumni Association President, said: "We get so stuck in a rut with the things we do and the decisions we make that we don't realize there are other alternatives from which we can choose."

The lesson is to always be learning and to be open to new experiences. This will open up new files in your brain and help you see the world in a different way. In turn, it will enable you to have a much broader range of choices to make, which will be based on a much more enriched view of the world.

If you see Eddie or Mike, be sure to mention it to them.

Think Outside The Box

There are a couple of puzzles I use to introduce this principle. The first one is in Figure 9.

Figure 9

Your instructions are to add five lines to these six lines to make nine. Give it a try. Can you figure it out? I will let you toil with this for a few minutes and then I'll give you a hint.

Are you ready for your hint? When it says, "add five lines to these six lines to make nine," what is your mind thinking? Numbers and counting, right? It seems impossible because $5 + 6 = 11$, not 9. Does it become easier if I say to not think numbers and counting, but to think letters and words? You figured it out, didn't you? It's quite easy to see now.

NINE

Figure 10

That's right, adding five lines makes NINE.

Our brains are amazing in their capacity, but the trick is to use our brains in the right way, to organize and to look at information in different ways, and not get stuck seeing things the same old way, the way we have been conditioned to see things.

We can apply this in many aspects of our lives. In my anger management work with adolescents, I ask what makes them angry. They often tell me, "When someone calls me (insert any derogatory term here)." I ask them what happens when someone calls them that name. They frequently say, "I call them a name back." Sometimes they report becoming aggressive and even violent, especially if "they say something about my Mama!"

I then apply the little NINE puzzle. I ask them if they can see the situation in any other way that would lead them to not be angry, like shifting our thinking from *numbers* to *letters*. Inevitably some of them will recognize that they don't have to respond in the same old way and call the person a name back but can simply smile and walk away.

Falling back on the basic premise of this book, the change that enables us to not become angry and to respond differently is in our thinking.

We will respond to name calling the same old way if we think the same old way about being called a name, the same old way we've been trained to think. And we will wonder why we are the same old angry.

I ask them to stop thinking *numbers and counting* and begin thinking *letters and words*. When someone calls them a name, instead of thinking, "How dare they; they can't do that; they're disrespecting me and I cannot let that happen," they can think, "That's kind of stupid; who cares; that person is immature; it's not even worth my time."

As they switch their thinking, they see the situation differently and it becomes easier to respond in a different way.

Let's apply this principle to another situation.

Someone where you work is negative and hostile. The same old way of responding may be to give negativity and hostility back to them or to not do anything but let it ruin your day by stewing about it even after you get home.

You're stuck thinking *numbers and counting* so when they are negative you think, "That person is a jerk; I can't stand him; he makes me miserable."

Thinking outside the box would lead you to think, "There he goes again; that's his style; oh well, life goes on; I won't let him ruin my day." Maybe you could even try smiling at him and being friendly.

That would be a much different way of responding and could very possibly lead to a far different outcome in the short-term and in the long-term.

The next image, the famous Nine Dots Puzzle, is where the phrase "think outside the box" originated in 1914.

Look at Figure 11.

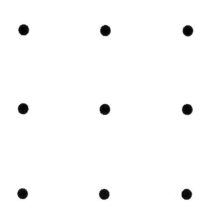

Figure 11

The instructions are to connect all the dots using only four straight lines. You cannot lift your pen and you cannot retrace your lines. That's it. Go for it. I'll give you a few minutes and then I'll give you a hint.

Before I give you a hint, remember how the human mind works. The brain is a magnificent organ that holds information and enables us to be efficient and accomplish so much in our lives.

The efficiency of our mind is a great asset, but it can be a liability if we don't organize our information well or if we are too rigid in how we file it. For example, look at these simple marks and what do you see?

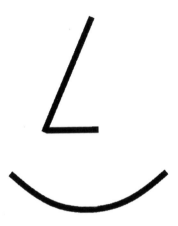

Figure 12

Most people say it looks like a face, a nose and a mouth. We probably have all doodled like this to make a face. But is it really a face? Where are the eyes and eyebrows? Where are the cheeks? How about the chin?

So much is missing but our efficient mind takes a little information and fills in the blanks to make sense of what we see. This usually is a good thing, allowing us to be more efficient in daily life; however, it can be a bad thing, too.

It's bad when we fill the blanks in wrong and when what we thought turns out to be something very different.

If you thought the lines made a face, take a look at the next figure to see what it really is.

Figure 13

It's a sailboat here, but it could be something else if we took time to fill the blanks in differently.

So now back to our dots puzzle in Figure 11. What do you see when you look at those nine dots?

Because they are symmetrical, most people see a square or a box, so most of us attempt to solve the puzzle by staying *inside the box*. Right?

The hint is to think outside the box. Often, even after I give the hint, people continue trying to solve the puzzle by staying inside the imagined box. I tell them there is no box, except the one that exists in their heads.

Our minds can be so stubborn at times that they resist change, even when the solution is pointed out. We become so efficient and function on automatic pilot so often that it can be harmful.

See if you can solve the puzzle now. Remember to think outside the box, beyond the imaginary square that exists in your head. If you can't figure it out, look at the next figure for the answer.

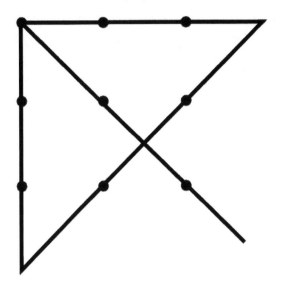

Figure 14

Well, what do you think? Does that work? It accomplished the objective of connecting all the dots with four straight lines, without lifting the pen or retracing any lines. Often, when I finally show the answer, people say, "You cheated, you went outside the box." You know what I say, right? "Box? What box? There is no box. The only box is the one that exists inside your head." Even after discussing this in depth, some people still have a difficult time reprogramming their brain to see it differently.

Again, let's apply this to life. If our mind is so stuck seeing things the same old way in a little puzzle *even after telling it to see things differently*, imagine how years of thinking a certain way, seeing things a certain way, and behaving a certain way can leave us stuck that way and take such great effort to pry us out.

Let's look at another example of thinking outside the box, and remember that staying inside the box can be narrow-minded thinking. It's looking at things, people, or situations the same old way. It's narrow-mindedness. The patterns of behavior that follow are typically problematic.

Some people *always* get mad if someone calls them a name or is perceived as being mean to them. They hold a grudge and desire to get revenge. They can't see it any other way. If you ask them to think outside the box, they could say, "Instead of hitting them with my fist I could hit them with a bat." They don't realize that they can choose to think about the situation differently, in such way that they don't even become angry. In a situation where someone called them a name or was vulgar and demeaning to them, instead of retaliation they could respond with respect or patience or kindness. As they do this, there is a high likelihood that patterns of interaction will change and any negativity or hostility will dissipate.

Section 2—How Perception Creates Reality

Here is an example of thinking outside the box and ultimately acting differently than what might be expected.

Jack, a teenage boy, lost his father to cancer. He and his mother faced financial hardships and had to move to a different town. Jack was the new kid in school and was depressed, which led to bullying by some of his peers. Inside-the-box thinking is, "My life stinks; I have no friends; these kids are all jerks; I'll never get past this; I just want to crawl under a rock." The behavior that follows this is withdrawal, isolation, or possibly hostility and aggression. Those behaviors would simply perpetuate the problem.

However, Jack chose to think outside the box: "I'm not going to stoop to their level; I can get past this; I can make friends here; this is hard but I will succeed." At the main entrance of his school every morning, he held the door open for hundreds of his classmates coming in for class. In no time, most of the kids came to know him as the new, polite kid who held the door for everyone before school started. The bullying stopped and he had a bunch of friends plus the potential for many more.

Are there aspects of your life that are unfulfilling and even distressing? Are you stuck waiting for some element to change or some person to change or perhaps move away? Stretch yourself a bit. Consider changing old ways of thinking that keep you stuck in old patterns of behavior that are self-defeating and not allowing you to move forward successfully.

Mediating Variables And Other Challenges

The graph in Figure 15 looks at two variables, Life Challenges on the X axis and Life Satisfaction on the Y axis. Each axis goes from 0 to 100.

Place a point on this graph where you believe you would fall as you carefully consider the life challenges you have experienced and the amount of life satisfaction you enjoy.

You can do this little exercise in a group with coworkers or friends just to see the pattern that emerges. I have done this for years with adolescents and have observed a variety of patterns.

The discussions that follow are always stimulating.

Figure 15

If I stopped people in the street and asked if they believe there is a relationship between life challenges and life satisfaction, what would they say? What would you say?

The majority of people believe there is a negative relationship, meaning that as life challenges go up, life satisfaction goes down.

Is that what you believe? If so, our graph would look something like Figure 16.

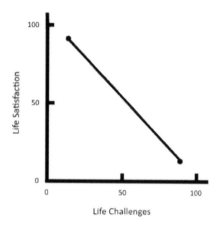

Figure 16

Many times as I have done this exercise in groups, the table has looked like this.

However, many times it has looked more like Figure 17.

The relationship between life challenges and life satisfaction suggested by Figure 17 is a positive correlation, or, in other words, as one variable goes up the other variable goes up with it.

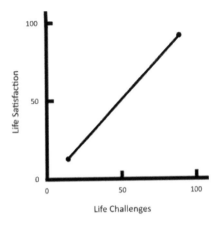

Figure 17

Finally, often the graph looks like Figure 18. This graph suggests there is no relationship between these two variables and that everyone is different.

For some, the more life challenges they face the less life satisfaction they experience, while with others, the more challenges, the greater the life satisfaction.

Figure 18 is more typical of the general population, suggesting there is no direct relationship between these two variables.

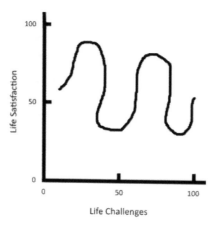

Figure 18

However, I believe there is a relationship between these two variables, but it is determined by a third or *mediating* variable. There actually may be two or three mediating variables that influence how life challenges influence life satisfaction. These variables are related to earlier chapters of this book, as you will see.

To illustrate the first mediating variable, let's use a scenario with two teenage girls, Lisa and Diane, both of whom experienced sexual abuse as children. The abuse was about the same frequency and duration for each girl. When we plot their points on the graph, we notice that Lisa is 90 on the life challenges axis and 10 on the life satisfaction axis. Diane is also 90 on the life challenges axis but, surprisingly, is 90 on the life satisfaction axis. How can that be? They both rated themselves the same on life challenges but one is quite happy with her life and the other is not. The first and most significant mediating variable is *perception*.

We discussed perception earlier and will talk about it again. In fact, if one word could describe what this book is about, it would be the importance of *perception*. We can look at the facts of a situation and measure times and distances and many other variables and there could be no disputing the facts. However, the perception, or how we view those facts, may be very different and is completely up to each of us.

So, back to Lisa and Diane.

How did Lisa look at the abuse that led to her low life satisfaction? She probably felt it was her fault, that she is a bad person because it happened, that she is broken and her life is ruined. Are any of these perceptions accurate? Are any of these perceptions *rational?* Rational means logical, sensible, or reasonable. As an outside observer, you would say no, of course not, her perceptions are totally irrational. But to Lisa, they are absolutely real. She has no idea that she has chosen to think this way.

Can you see why her life satisfaction is so low? Put yourself in Lisa's shoes and choose those thoughts. How does that make you feel? Do you feel good about yourself? Do you have much hope for the future? How do you go about your daily life, with enthusiasm and determination or with isolation and hopelessness? As we approach life with isolation and hopelessness, what happens?

Now you see how these negative perceptions as a foundation for life only exacerbate the problem and lead to more hopelessness and depression and more dissatisfaction with life.

Now let's look at Diane. Her perceptions of the abuse are that it was awful, that she is glad it's over, but it wasn't her fault. She is not broken and her life is not ruined but is still hers to manage. Having chosen these thoughts, how does Diane feel about her life? She seems hopeful, excited, and determined to move forward and be successful. With these feelings, what direction will Diane's life take? She is likely to get the help she needs, to engage in productive activities, to take charge, and experience much success and ultimately much higher life satisfaction.

Let's look at a second mediating variable. If you were busy helping someone with a problem or project or were focused in some way on accomplishing something for someone else, especially if you sincerely cared about them, you are less likely to feel upset or depressed about yourself. In that moment, you are concentrating on that person and doing something for them. That person feels better because of your support and, importantly, you feel better because you were helpful and engaged in a worthwhile project. The second mediating variable that impacts how life challenges and life satisfaction relate is *getting outside yourself.*

When we are not thinking about our problems, challenges, or life stressors, but are genuinely intent on helping and serving someone else, no matter how big or small or for how long, we cannot be as down on ourselves. I realize there are some issues that cannot be ignored and need time and attention, but they rarely need 24/7 time and attention. You have to eat and sleep and bathe, right? In the course of your day, it is wise to allot some time to helping others, which ultimately will help lift you.

The third mediating variable is *forward thinking.* No one is immune to the challenges that life brings. Whenever we face a challenge, it is common for us to become immersed in the moment and forget there is so much more to life that lies ahead. We must be able to look beyond the current difficulty, to look to the future, and continue with great anticipation for many extraordinary future life events.

Look back to a significant challenge you have faced. Remember how you felt as you contemplated the gravity of this challenge and wondered how you were ever going to overcome it and move forward with life. You had your doubts, but somehow you slowly but surely moved forward with life. You may have slowed down some plans or modified them, but look at you now. You're living life and possibly doing even better than you ever would have expected. Perhaps in hindsight the challenge doesn't look so ominous. Perhaps you've had many significant challenges in the ensuing years that have caused this original challenge to not seem so overwhelming.

So, when dealing with any life challenge, remember these three mediating variables: *perception*, *getting outside yourself*, and *forward thinking*. This will enable you to face your challenges and be strengthened by them rather than having them knock you down and be weakened because of them.

Section 3—Selfie-Perception

Sunken Treasure: The Iceberg Theory Of Human Behavior

I Think I Can, I Think I Can And Other Self-Fulfilling Prophecies

Sunken Treasure: The Iceberg Theory of Human Behavior

An iceberg is one of nature's most beautiful and fascinating phenomena, with unusual properties. Whether we have seen an iceberg in person or in pictures, it is easy to believe we have seen most of it. However, this is not true and is actually part of the sad story of the tragedy of the unsinkable *RMS Titanic.* The majority of the iceberg is unseen below the surface. What we see above the water is only about 10 percent of the total iceberg. The next time you have a glass of ice water, take note of the ice cubes. Little of the ice cube is actually above the surface of the water. The whole ice cube is floating but most of it lies below the surface.

So what does this have to do with human behavior? All of us have a public self and a private self. The public self is the part of ourselves we display to people at work, school, church, the mall, or any number of public places. We typically put our best foot forward, so to speak. We dress neatly, brush our teeth, comb our hair, and our behavior is generally more polite and refined.

Our private self is the part of ourselves that we display at home around family and perhaps close friends. We aren't as concerned with dressing just right or doing our hair and makeup. We can just be ourselves, much less formal, and let our perceived shortcomings be seen. We are often not as careful with our words or behaviors, primarily because we do not fear judgment as much from individuals within our inner circle of family and friends.

Now, let's relate this to icebergs. As you probably have figured out, the part of the iceberg that sits on top of the water represents our public self, while the part of the iceberg that sits below the surface, the biggest part that few people see, represents our private self. The theory then relates to perceptions and self-image. When we are out in public, we see other people's public self, but typically do not see what is below the surface, the private self. So we see their best but smallest part.

Because we don't often see the other, less than ideal part of most people, we can forget they have that part. We assume they have no problems or shortcomings and really have their lives together. The problem is that we compare their best 10 percent with our worst 90 percent, so we always fall far short by comparison. This is obviously unfair and we will always lose. This is what drives those who have low self-esteem to continue to believe they are defective or deficient compared to others. They stay stuck in their hypotheses that they are not a good person.

I once worked with a young woman who came to the hospital suffering from severe depression with suicidal thoughts. When I first met with Jan, to question why she was so depressed and wanted to hurt herself, she adamantly insisted that she was a "bad person." When I asked how she determined that she was a bad person, she declared that she had done a lot of "bad things." I suggested that I had done bad things, too. She disputed this and claimed she had done "really bad things" and, despite my pressing her, believed she had not done any "good things." She believed that the other patients on the unit and, in fact, most everyone in the world, was a better person than she was. I invited her to play a game with me. After the game, I explained what we learn from it.

The way the game works is I name a skill or talent or personality characteristic and each person in the group gives themselves a score from 0, really horrible, to 10, great at it. I start with something like singing and everyone gives themselves a score. Next comes cooking and then dancing, math, writing, playing basketball, being friendly, sense of humor, reliability, and so on. As we play, we notice there are times when each of us scored quite low, times when we each scored quite high, and times when we were somewhere in the middle.

As we finish the game, I say we are now going to write down the average score for each player. I ask to see if they can figure out what the average score is going to be for each person. After thinking a bit, the answer often comes, a 5. This is absolutely true. We are all just a 5, no better, no worse. We are all just a bunch of humans with strengths and weaknesses and no one is better at "being a person" than anyone else. We are all simply human.

To believe that someone is a better person than you is to suggest that of the seven billion people in the world, there is someone who is Number 1, the best, and Number 2, second best, and Number 3, all the way down to Number 7,000,000,000, the worst. No one wants to sit next to that guy on the bus, right? No, the notion is absurd. It simply does not work that way. Again, no one is better at "being a person" than anybody else. We are all just humans and someone may be better at cooking than you are but you may be better at singing than someone else.

Here is another way to look at it. Two people are with me and I want you to decide which person has more worth. Greg is a neurosurgeon who stands 5' 6" and weighs 130 pounds. Butch is a felon who has been incarcerated for robbery and assault, who stands 6' 5" and weighs 250 pounds. Most people would say, of course, the neurosurgeon has more worth than the felon.

Remember the little game above, however, and the point that no one is a better person than anyone else. Just because someone has done bad things doesn't mean they are a bad person. After all, we have all done bad things. People can change and stop doing bad things and do more good things. If we break each person down into a number of different areas and realize that everyone has strengths and weaknesses, we know that, ultimately, we all average out to a 5.

If your car slid off the road into a snowbank and you needed to push it out, which person would be of more worth to you, the scrawny neurosurgeon or the muscular felon? What if you needed a bass singer to round out your choir? Perhaps the big felon has a nice bass voice. What if you needed a center for your basketball team? The big, tall felon would certainly be of more worth to you.

So how do you see yourself? We already know you are a 5 just like everyone else. That's neither a good thing nor a bad thing, it just is, so stop worrying about how you rate with the rest of the world. Decide what is important to you and focus on that.

Keep in mind you are not comparing yourself to others. You may feel that being good at playing the violin is really important to you, so work at it. Practice regularly and you will improve. You will find joy. Don't get down on yourself because some other kid is first chair in the school orchestra and plays better than you. You're not playing the violin to be better than her. This kind of comparison doesn't bring joy but can breed hard feelings and potentially a dislike for playing the violin.

Practice because you want to get better for you and your family and you can experience the joy and satisfaction of playing different pieces even if they are not perfect.

I Think I Can, I Think I Can And Other Self-Fulfilling Prophecies

In 1968, during a time of discord about race and desegregation in the United States, Jane Elliott, a teacher in Iowa decided to teach her third-grade students a lesson about segregation and racism and the human experience in general. She came to class one day and told the children that blue-eyed students are smarter than brown-eyed students so she was going to give the blue-eyed students special privileges that the brown-eyed students would not receive. She spent time with the blue-eyed students and practiced vocabulary and math with flash cards. She timed them on these exercises so she would have a baseline from which to judge. She then worked with the brown-eyed students on the same vocabulary and math with flash cards and timed them. She compared the times of the blue-eyed students with the brown-eyed students and discovered that the blue-eyed students performed better and faster than the brown-eyed students.

The next week she announced a correction, that brown-eyed students were actually smarter than the blue-eyed students. Consequently, the brown-eyed students would receive special privileges and the blue-eyed students would not. Like the previous week, she worked with both sets of students on vocabulary and math with flashcards and timed them. The blue-eyed students performed much more slowly than the week before. Conversely, the brown-eyed students, having been told they were smarter, scored much better in the second week. When the teacher asked her students to write about this experience, many of them specifically mentioned how different they felt about themselves, good and bad, when the teacher explained to them about their eye colors.

Much can be learned from this simple classroom experiment. One thing it teaches us, which relates directly to what we address in this chapter, has to do with self-fulfilling prophecy. Why did the blue-eyed students perform more slowly when they were told they were not as smart as the brown-eyed students? Did their brains change overnight? Did they really get dumber the second week? What was the cause of their performance change? Students performed differently depending on which group they were in and their performances changed from one week to the next as their perception of their group and their own abilities changed. Somehow what they thought of themselves translated into behavior change and ultimately a difference in level of performance. We can broaden this to many different circumstances in life.

Here is another fascinating example that helps illustrate self-fulfilling prophecy. On May 6, 1954, a remarkable feat occurred. A man named Roger Bannister did something that no one had ever done. In fact, it was thought to be impossible for any human to run a mile in less than four minutes. The paradigm was that it was simply impossible to run that distance in any time shorter than 4:00. In 1945, a runner had come close with a time of 4:01.4. Then Bannister ran the mile in 3:59.4 seconds, forever breaking the four-minute mile barrier.

Running a mile as fast as Roger Bannister did was an astonishing feat. As a behavioral scientist, though, what is even more amazing to me is what happened after Bannister broke the unbreakable barrier. Just six weeks later, John Landy broke the 4-minute mile, and a few weeks later Roger and John both ran another mile in less than four minutes. Within the next year, more people broke the 4-minute mile. Within a few years, many runners had repeated Bannister's accomplishment.

So how did this happen? This makes for a fascinating study of human behavior. Some suggest that technology, training, and nutrition improved to make it possible for so many to break this record. Sixty years later, when more than 1,300 runners have broken the 4-minute mile mark, there is some validity to the technology, training, nutrition argument, but it couldn't explain the immediate change over just six weeks.

Once the undoable feat had been done, it was done again and again in a very short time. There are other factors involved, with the main one being self-fulfilling prophecy. Before Bannister broke the record, it was truly believed that no one could do it. The paradigm that no one could run that fast was proven to be false. It became humanly possible for someone to run faster than a 4-minute mile, and people thought if he could do it why not me? Once it was believed, or once runners got rid of the mental block that it couldn't be done, they started to run that fast. Their belief translated into action and their bodies started to run just a little faster, just 1 or 2 seconds faster, which was all it required. The human body can do amazing things if it believes it can and is not hindered by false beliefs that impact our physical, mental, and intellectual capacities.

Let's consider the example of Eric, a teenage boy. His parents announce they are moving from the small town in Missouri where they have lived most of his life, to the big city of St. Louis. Eric is upset and tells his parents he does not want to live in St. Louis because he hates St. Louis. He doesn't know anybody there and will not have any friends. Despite his pleadings, the parents inform him that because of his father's work they will move.

Fast forward two months. The family has moved to St. Louis, and Eric sits on his front steps in a suburb as the moving crew unloads furniture into their new home. Sitting there with his head in his hands, two teenage boys walk down the street bouncing a basketball. As they approach Eric they shout, "Hey, you moving in?" He replies glumly, "yeah." The boys ask if he wants to play basketball, but he says no and the boys go on their way. Soon another young man walks by and says hello. Eric just sits and says nothing to the neighbor, who walks on. A little later, a neighbor boy walks by and asks if he is moving into the neighborhood. Eric says yes but keeps his head down. The neighbor asks his name and welcomes him to the neighborhood and then walks away.

Later that evening, while eating dinner with his parents, Eric says, "I hate St. Louis; I told you I wasn't going to have any friends here." What happened? Was it inevitable that Eric was not going to have any friends in St. Louis? We could jump ahead a month or two and predict what might happen if Eric continues this pattern of isolating himself and letting opportunities to make friends pass by. He goes to school and can't wait until the closing bell to get home and doesn't even entertain the possibility of joining a club, a team, or the band. Instead, he returns home, secluding himself in his bedroom, and plays video games until his mother calls him to dinner.

So Eric was right, he has no friends in St. Louis, as he predicted. How did he know? This is the principle we are talking about, self-fulfilling prophecy, and it relates to a larger principle in life, constructivism vs. fatalism. Do you *let* life happen to you or do you *make* life happen? Was Eric destined to have no friends in St. Louis, or is it really up to him whether he has friends there? I think you know the answer because the example makes it obvious, but there are many other scenarios in people's lives that aren't quite so obvious.

Let's consider another example about education and going to college. Many people think school is a real drag and they are simply not cut out for it. They will never go to college because that is simply impossible.

They are not college material. So here's how it plays out for one young man.

Calvin is 14 years old, starting his freshman year in high school. Through middle school, he was a B and C student, not a Brainiac but not stupid. He never really liked math and science and the first semester of his freshman year he is enrolled in Algebra. He says to family and friends, "Algebra is going to be really hard and I'll probably flunk." Can you see the prophecy he has just made?

The first day of class comes and this thought, this prophecy, is in the back of his mind. Calvin listens to the teacher and almost immediately gets bored and his mind starts to wander. He says to himself, "I was right. This is hard and it's really boring, too." His mind wanders more and he starts to doodle in his notebook. The bell finally rings and he feels relieved that he is out of Algebra class. Subsequent classes the rest of the week are no better than that first day. In fact, they are worse because his prophecy is becoming more and more ingrained.

A quiz is announced for the end of the week. Calvin is sure he will flunk because, "Algebra is hard and I can't do it." He did homework half-heartedly because he hasn't paid attention in class and doesn't understand the concepts that were taught. He comes to class on Friday to take the quiz and does poorly, just as he predicted. As the semester progresses, Calvin continues to think Algebra is really hard and his mind is not meant to understand it. Not only does he stop paying attention in class but he starts skipping a day or two a week so he completely solidifies his failing grade at the end of the semester.

Calvin treats his science class the same way and the outcome is the same. As he approaches his sophomore year with half the credits he could or should have, his peers begin to look ahead and talk about college. He tells some friends, "I'm not going to go to college. College is for the brains."

Do you see another prophecy and recognize how prophecies easily and naturally build on one another? He proceeds through his sophomore year following the same pattern of his freshman year, not paying attention in class because he knows he won't understand the material and eventually he skips class and ultimately receives another failing grade. By the time his junior year rolls around, he is even farther behind his peers with little hope of catching up. He is ready to throw in the towel.

Even before Christmas vacation starts, Calvin has dropped out with no intention of completing his high school education. A couple of years pass as he works in a local fast food restaurant. Some old high school classmates come home from college for the holidays and stop in to grab a bite to eat. He chats with them and asks them how they like college. He says to them, "I told you I wasn't going to go to college."

Calvin is sure that he was not supposed to go to college. If we stop and examine what really happened it seems obvious from our perspective. It wasn't written in the stars. Rather, he made it happen by first making a prophecy and then going about fulfilling that prophecy with his beliefs and actions every day.

The wonderful thing about self-fulfilling prophecy is that it not only works *against* people but if you understand the concept it can work *for* you. Consider Eric who moved to St. Louis. He could have said, "St Louis is a big city with lots of people; I'll certainly be able to make a lot of friends." Thinking this, sitting on his steps the day of the move, he jumps at the invitation to play basketball and makes not only two new friends but nine new friends when he includes all the others already at the courts. By simply recognizing that he *makes* life happen rather than *waiting* for life to happen, the outcome is quite different and much more positive.

What prophecies have you made that have limited you? What prophecies are you continuing to make that you need to change? What new prophecies can you make that will work to your advantage?

Section 4—You Are In Charge

Your Thoughts Are Key To Life Management

You Decide What You Feel And How You Behave

Good Place, Bad Place, You Create Your World

You Gotta Deal With Difficult People

Your Thoughts Are Key To Life Management

Many people spend their lives trying to figure out how to manage the ups and downs of life, negotiating the challenges of interpersonal relationships, and navigating the complexities of various career paths.

They can be very intelligent, have a great deal of skill in their chosen field, be charismatic, attractive, and even wealthy, but, if they do not understand this one principle, they will never successfully manage the various aspects of their lives.

Many people believe that events determine how they feel and behave and essentially drive their lives. Figure 19 illustrates this point.

Figure 19

Let's plug in a couple of situations.

Suppose someone gossips about you. That's an event. In most people, that would cause feelings of anger or hurt, possibly followed by retaliation or other hostile behavior, or maybe withdrawn, isolating behavior. Ultimately, the outcome is low self-esteem and, in the long run, maybe few friends.

Here's another event which is more difficult, the breakup of a relationship. For many people, that would result in feelings of sadness, depression, and hopelessness. The resulting behavior likely would be to withdraw and not seek to meet others. The outcome would be no new relationship and low self-esteem.

Is this how it works? No, absolutely not. You probably realize that this pattern isn't how it happens because you have approached many events differently throughout your life, resulting in a more positive outcome.

Look at Figure 20, because this is how it really works. Figure 19 left out the most important step in the process, the one that comes right between the event and the feeling: thoughts.

Figure 20

I tell patients that this is the most important thing they can learn during their time in the hospital, the most important thing they can learn in all their treatment, the most important thing they can learn in all their schooling, the most important thing they can learn throughout their lives. If you can understand this principle, you will be head and shoulders above so many others in life. You will have learned the secret to making life happen instead of letting life happen to you.

You can go back to the earlier examples and add this all-important step: thoughts. The key to this whole process with this additional step is that *you get to choose your thoughts.* An event has no power to create a feeling. The feeling only comes after you have processed the event in your mind and have chosen various thoughts to apply to the event.

Take the example of someone gossiping about you. Remember, the event does not, and cannot, create a feeling, but rather your choice of thoughts creates feelings. What types of thoughts would create the feeling of anger or hurt? "How dare he gossip like that." "He can't say that about me." "I'll show him." "Everyone always picks on me." "Nobody likes me."

Can you see how choosing such thoughts would lead to anger or hurt? The behavior that follows is pretty well set in motion because of the thought choice.

Now, the part of this principle that must be understood is that there are only two types of thoughts. They are not right or wrong, good or bad, positive or negative. They are simply *rational* or *irrational*.

To help you understand, let me ask if you can think of a good or positive thought about a tornado destroying a town and killing many people. How about a good or positive thought about a tragedy like a school shooting? No way, right? But no matter what the situation, you can choose rational thoughts. So, what does rational mean? It means sensible, reasonable, or logical. Therefore, irrational obviously means not sensible, unreasonable, or illogical. Which type of thoughts would you rather have? The answer, rational thoughts, should be obvious, right?

This is such a powerful principle to understand and apply in life. Your day-to-day experience will be so much more fulfilling and you will feel in control of your life as you apply this. Don't misunderstand, though. This principle is not magic and does not have the ability to make you happy all the time and to never become upset or angry. Sad or angry emotions are a natural and essential part of the human experience.

What you need to do is explore the thoughts you have chosen in any given situation and determine whether they are rational or irrational. If they are rational, you can know and feel confident that the feelings that follow are a natural and appropriate part of life. If the thoughts you choose are irrational, the feelings that follow are not natural and you do not need to experience those feelings. Instead, you need to go back and rework your thoughts to make sure they are rational.

Now that you have learned something about rational and irrational thoughts, let's see if the thoughts that were chosen following the gossip are rational or irrational.

"How dare he gossip like that." The fact is he did say it and he can say that if he wants. This is an irrational thought.

"He can't say that about me." Once again, he *can* say that and he did, and he can say many other things if he chooses. This is an irrational thought.

"I'll show him." You can try to be big and bad, but if you think you're going to go through life always

103

forcing people to stop doing things you don't like, it's going to be a long and difficult life. This is an irrational thought.

"Everyone always picks on me." Everyone means *everyone*. Really? Everyone? All your neighbors, all your friends, all your family members, all your peers at school, all your teachers, all your coworkers, the guy behind the counter at Wendy's? I think you get the idea. This is a really irrational thought.

"Nobody likes me." Nobody means *nobody*. You're saying that none of your neighbors like you, none of your friends like you, none of your family members like you, none of your peers at school or your teachers like you, and none of your coworkers like you. Again, obviously, this is an irrational thought.

Let's try replacing these irrational thoughts with rational ones.

"Wow, he's immature. I don't have to pay any attention to that."

"I know I'm not (insert any gossipy phrase here). I'll just go on my way."

"He must be having a bad day and I'm just the target right now."

"Oh well, this is not the first time I've been gossiped about. This will pass"

Now let's consider the feelings that follow these rational thoughts. They are quite different from the feelings that follow irrational thoughts. Feelings might include being a little annoyed but are more likely to be indifferent and mellow. The behavior that follows is to ignore, to walk away, and to continue on with little disruption. The outcome, ultimately, is no problem. Life goes on almost as if nothing ever happened.

Let's apply this to a common but much more difficult life experience, the death of a loved one. Plug this experience into the flow chart in Figure 20, where thoughts follow the event. As stated earlier, we often believe feelings come from an event. The feelings many of my patients have following such a loss are hopelessness and depression. The behaviors that often follow these feelings are isolation, substance abuse, self-harm, even suicidal ideation. The outcome to these behaviors could be continued depression, hospitalization, or even death.

Now, let's go back and fill in the thoughts that were chosen that actually lead to the feelings, because, remember, the event has no power to create feelings. Our mind is operating and we choose to think certain thoughts. The thoughts that lead to hopelessness and depression would be "I need him." "I can't live without him." "I'll never be happy ever again."

Okay. Are these thoughts rational or irrational? Obviously, they are not sensible or logical, are they. I don't mean to seem cold or heartless, but we need air and water and food: we don't need another person to live. To say we'll never be happy again, we would need a crystal ball that could show that in 40 years we are still not happy about anything in life.

You can see that this simply is not reasonable. Remember, I'm not suggesting I can make you happy all the time with whatever happens because that is simply not true. I can, however, help you navigate through your life experiences and approach them in a much more emotionally healthy fashion so that you won't experience severe depression.

Let's think of rational thoughts we can choose in place of the irrational thoughts. "This is very difficult." "I am really going to miss him." "I won't be able to spend time with him anymore." "I'll cherish the times I had with him." "He would not want me to be self-destructive." "I'll make my life a tribute to him." "I'll appreciate even more the relationships I have with loved ones now."

Having chosen these rational thoughts, are hopelessness and depression likely to follow? I think not. Sadness will still be one of your feelings, but not hopelessness, not depression, not wanting to die. There may be hope along with the sadness. As you are appropriately sad but have hope, what behavior will follow? Rather than self-destructive behaviors, we see constructive behaviors that will likely help us move through the difficult experience. The outcome will not be hospitalization and possible death but would be receiving support, increased emotional health, and possibly improved relationships with loved ones.

However difficult the experience, you always have a choice to choose rational or irrational thoughts. As we begin to manage our thoughts, as we choose to think more rationally, we ultimately manage our feelings and our behaviors, and the outcomes lead to a much healthier life.

You Decide What You Feel And What You Do

Every day I witness people who seem to believe they have little control over the outcome of their day and ultimately their life. They go along and let the world and people in it dictate whether they have a good day. They wander aimlessly through life with little hope for happiness and fulfillment. I compare these people to pinballs in a pinball machine. How much control does a pinball have over where it goes? The flippers and bumpers and gravity decide where it goes, the pinball simply reacts to its environment. Pinball people are reactive and let others determine their actions, their moods, and ultimately, the course their life takes.

With many of my patients, if someone calls them a name they get angry and call them a name back. They don't think they have options to control the situation. They react and ultimately give control to the other person. They allow outside forces to dictate how they feel and what they do. What they fail to understand is that they can take control of the situation and be proactive.

Do not allow forces outside of you to dictate how you feel or what you do, but rather ensure that *you* decide what you feel and how you behave. You can decide what to do regardless of what someone else does. The locus of control is within you and not out in the world.

When I think of this principle, I think of a story about a young man who truly understood how this worked and applied it in his life. You may have heard of the Broadway play *Joseph and the Amazing Technicolor Dreamcoat*, which is based on a Bible story. Joseph was the youngest of many brothers but was favored by his father, who made him a colorful cloak. The older brothers were jealous of Joseph and one wanted to kill him. The oldest brother persuaded him not to kill Joseph but to sell him as a slave, which they eventually did to a group of Midianites traveling through Israel. The brothers took Joseph's cloak, smeared lamb's blood on it, and took it to their father saying that a mountain lion must have killed Joseph as he was tending the flocks.

Before we continue the story, let me ask how you would feel if your own siblings sold you as a slave. I'd be more than a little upset and have a good reason to say, "My life stinks. This is totally unfair." Let's see how Joseph dealt with this, whether he was reactive or proactive.

Joseph traveled with the Midianites down to Egypt where he was again sold as a slave to a wealthy and important person named Potiphar. Potiphar was the Pharaoh's head general, a powerful man with a large estate and many servants. Joseph could have dragged his feet and been a real problem slave and even tried to run off, but he decided to stay and work hard. He worked so intently that Potiphar put him in charge of his whole estate. Not a bad gig, huh? Joseph was moving up and things were not so bad.

Well, once again, life happened, things Joseph couldn't control. Potiphar's wife liked Joseph. She had him come to her bedchamber and wanted him to lie with her. Joseph wanted absolutely nothing to do with that and he fled. Potiphar's wife was offended that Joseph had no desire for her and lied to her husband, saying that Joseph tried to come on to her. As a result, Potiphar had Joseph put in prison. If you were in Joseph's shoes, would you be just a little discouraged, thinking life isn't treating you fairly? Most people in Joseph's place would be upset and angry with the injustice of it all.

As the story continued, Joseph, who had every reason to be negative and uncooperative, decided to be proactive and work hard. In doing so, the head warden observed Joseph and was impressed with his attitude and work ethic to the degree that he put Joseph in charge of the whole prison. Here he was, a prisoner, probably at one of the lowest points of his life, and now he's climbing up again and making something out of an unfair and seemingly hopeless situation.

Pharaoh, who was known to be harsh with his servants, had a couple of them committed to prison. While in prison, one of these servants had a dream and shared it with Joseph, who interpreted his dream. Word got back to Pharaoh that there was a guy in prison who could interpret dreams. Pharaoh had an elaborate dream he wanted to have interpreted, so he sent servants to retrieve Joseph and bring him to his quarters. Joseph happily obliged the Pharaoh and interpreted his dream.

Joseph told Pharaoh that the dream was a message to him to prepare for the future, that there were going to be seven years of plenty with much rain and good crops, followed by seven years of famine where there would be no rain and no crops. Joseph counseled Pharaoh that he needed to store up grain during the seven years of plenty in preparation for the seven years

111

of famine. After hearing Joseph's interpretation, Pharaoh was impressed and determined to do just as Joseph instructed.

As time passed, Egypt and her surrounding lands enjoyed plenty of rain and bounteous harvests until the seventh year, as Joseph predicted. A terrible drought hit the region and people struggled to harvest any crops. Fortunately, because of Joseph's interpretation and counsel to Pharaoh, Egypt was well-prepared. They were so well-prepared compared to the rest of the region that people from all around traveled to Egypt to obtain grain. Included in the throngs of people were Joseph's brothers.

As they came to Egypt to get food, the brothers had no idea who this man was doling out sacks of grain. It had been many years since Joseph was first sold and he had grown up and matured in the Egyptian culture. He now looked very different and his brothers did not recognize him, although he recognized them. He met a younger brother who was not born when Joseph was still with his family. Joseph longed to see his father and devised a plan. He hid a golden goblet in the youngest brother's sack of grain so that when he left one of the guards identified the boy as a thief. Joseph then stated that the boy could not leave and be reunited with his family until his father came to get him. The brothers complied with Joseph's demands and traveled back to Israel where they explained to their father what happened. Joseph's father and brothers traveled back to Egypt where Joseph revealed his true identity and forgave his brothers for selling him as a slave.

In the end, Joseph went from being a slave to being second in command only to Pharaoh in all the region because he chose to be proactive and not let other people and life circumstances control his mood, his attitude, and ultimately, his life.

Many people blame others for things that happen or for the mood in which they find themselves. I can't tell you how many times I have heard someone say, "He made me mad." I'm not suggesting we should never get mad because sometimes anger is appropriate, but can anyone else really make us mad? Ultimately, getting mad or not is our decision. What happens to us is often not up to us, but how we *choose* to respond is completely up to us. If someone is mean to you, does that make you mad or did you choose to become mad because of what you thought about what that person did?

You learned this in the previous chapter. Now, after we consider thought choices, we are going to focus on your interactions with the world. If you got mad, perhaps you chose to think something like this: "That was so mean. He can't do that. I need to get him back. I'll show him who he's dealing with." As you can see, your anger did not come from outside you because of what someone did, but rather from inside you from what you chose to think.

Let's look at other thoughts you could choose and consider the outcome. "Well, that was strange. What's up with this guy? He is pretty immature. He must be having a bad day. That's not even worth my time or attention." If you choose these thoughts, you wouldn't feel mad but indifferent. You realize it's mostly a reflection on him and has nothing to do with you, so ignoring it and going on is the best response.

Remember the pinball people? You can see how a person who reacts to the external environment is really choosing thoughts that cause anger without realizing it. People who have low self-esteem often have a more difficult time navigating through situations like being called a name because they have a deep-seated feeling of inadequacy that causes hurt and stirs emotions that are uncomfortable. These individuals have chosen these thoughts for these situations for so long they just click on a file they created many years ago. Every addition to the file only makes it harder to change.

One of the more important lessons we learn is that you cannot control anyone but yourself. You cannot make anyone do anything. You may think you can and that you have. You may threaten to beat up a peer at school or even a coworker. You may think of one who is intimidating to another or one in a position of authority over another. Yes, there are elements in many situations that might *compel* someone to do something they do not want to do, but *ultimately,* the person has the choice to do what you say. They may be okay with the consequences of being beaten up or being fired from their job, or they don't believe you will follow through with your threat. Someone may choose not to comply under extreme circumstances, perhaps even in a hostage situation, with a gun to his head, despite the possible consequence of losing his life.

Another example I often use is that of a little boy. Think of a two-year-old boy, perhaps your own child or a nephew or a brother. If he was coloring and a crayon was left on the floor, you could ask him to pick it up or even demand that he do it. But if he doesn't want to, can you make him pick it up? You may think you can make him pick it up because he knows you will swat his behind if he doesn't. Once again, the promise of force or some undesirable consequence is not always sufficient to make even a two-year-old act.

115

You could take his little hand in yours and force his fingers around the crayon and pick it up, but essentially, you are picking it up for him.

When my kids were little they sometimes would misbehave in a store such that I would need to take them outside. I would grab their hand and begin walking them toward the exit. They would resist but I would continue toward the door. Their resistance would culminate in what I call the wet noodle. The wet noodle is when the child's legs simply stop working and go limp, causing them to slide to the floor. No matter what you do, you cannot make them walk. When this happened, I would pick them up and carry them out to the car. It's comical now as I think back on it, but it illustrates this basic principle that so many people, young and old, do not understand. ***You can't control any other person and your attitude is dictated completely by you and not by anyone else.*** Because so many people don't understand this basic principle, they go through life being miserable because people aren't acting the way they want. No matter what we do, we cannot make people do what we want them to do.

Think of times when you have tried to get people to change so you would no longer be mad, upset, or frustrated. Perhaps you are still doing this right now and you don't even realize it. Perhaps you are holding a grudge towards someone or are in the midst of a conflict because someone does not respond the way you want. You believe you are right and they need to come to this realization and change in the way you want them to. Maybe you're right, maybe you're not. Maybe there is no right but rather two different opinions and you are trying to get something to happen over which you have no control. You can't change them, no matter how hard you try. Realize and accept that you cannot control anyone but yourself. Take charge of things over which you have control, your thoughts, and your behaviors. Life really is less stressful and much happier this way, I promise.

Good Place, Bad Place, You Create Your World

If you were to ask people what they think of the world, you would get a variety of answers. I often hear people say the world is a bad place full of mean people, a threatening place. Others, however, see people who are good and see much beauty in the world. The funny thing is that while they live in the same world they also live *in their own world, a world they have created.*

There is a fable of a wise old man who lived in a small town. When people considered moving to town but had questions about it, the townspeople always directed them to this wise man. One of the first questions they would ask was his opinion about the town. The man would always turn the question around and say, "Tell me about the last town in which you lived. Did you enjoy living there?" If the person said they disliked their town because the people were not friendly, the old man would say, "You're probably not going to like it here." If the person said they loved the town where they had lived because the people were so friendly and they were sad to be leaving, the old man would say, "I think you're going to like it here."

What was the wise man doing? Why did he respond with two different answers? Can you figure out the method to his madness? He knew that a town is a town and people are people, and no matter where you are, you determine what your experience will be like based on your thoughts and your behavior.

Here's a similar example I often use to illustrate this principle. This is not based on an actual story, but this phenomenon exists in every town across the country.

A family drives to town and sees a lady working in her yard. They pull over and say they are considering moving and want to know what she thinks of the people. She responds with an enthusiastic, "Oh, I love these people. They are so friendly and kind. Our neighbors are always watching out for us." The family asks about the school and teachers. The woman again responds with enthusiasm, "The school is great. The teachers really care about the kids and are very patient."

The family thanks the woman and drives a few blocks, where they see another woman outside her house. They pull over and ask her about the people who live

119

there, to which the woman responds with obvious disdain, "Oh, the people are not friendly at all and they're nosy and always in your business." The family is taken aback, given the contrast to what they had just learned from the first woman a few blocks away. They ask about the school and teachers. The woman, with added hostility, states, "The school hasn't been good for my kids. The teachers are self-centered and are only in it for the paycheck."

The family thanks the woman and drives away in bewilderment, wondering what just happened. Which woman is right? Whom do we believe?

Let's review this experience. Let's pretend this family has been your friends for many years and they call to tell you about their very confusing experience. They want to know what you think they should do about moving to this new town. What would you tell them? Which lady would you believe? If we take the old wise man's approach from the first story, how could you respond to this family?

The first lady likely is fairly open-minded and enjoys people. She smiles and says hello to people all over town as she passes them by. She reaches out to others and is fairly proactive in her life. She is often found at community events meeting new friends and helping out wherever she can. When she had smoke billowing over her house because grease from her grill caught fire, her neighbors came running over to see if she was okay. She was grateful for their concern. She taught her children good moral principles and social skills. She is firm but fair in her discipline of the children. If the teacher sends a note home about her child, she immediately believes what the teacher says and holds her child responsible for his behavior. Would you like for this woman to be your neighbor? Would you be her friend? She sounds like a great person who would make a great neighbor and would get along with almost anyone.

Let's look at the second woman. She is a negative person and stays to herself. She does not like getting involved with people because she doesn't trust them. They just hurt you. When she's around town she keeps her head down and doesn't talk to anybody. She doesn't participate in community events. When she had some smoke coming from her yard because she was burning leaves, the neighbors rushed over to check on her. She responded harshly and couldn't believe how nosy they were. She is inconsistent in teaching her children good moral principles and social skills, probably because she lacks some of these herself. Her discipline is generally permissive with random harsh punishments. When her child comes home with a note or she gets a call from the school for a behavior problem, she immediately gets defensive and decides the teachers and principal are out to get her kid, assuming her child is innocent. Would you like her to be your neighbor? Would you be her friend? It seems obvious, but she has a hard time getting along with people.

If you had a choice between her and the first woman, you would certainly choose the first woman to be your neighbor.

These two women live in the same town yet it is a very different place for each of them. It starts with their perceptions but quickly moves to their behaviors and ultimately the environment's response to each of them. Initially, it's the same town, the same people, the same school and teachers, but then it becomes a different town, different people, different school and teachers because of the feedback their worlds give each of them. They live in two different worlds that each woman has created.

You understand that whether a town is a nice place in which to live or not is by and large up to you. Towns are towns and people are people. These scenarios can be recreated in any town in the country or, for that matter, any school, any church, or any workplace. You have seen it, haven't you?

Here's a personal experience that illustrates this principle. In graduate school, I had an assistantship that earned a little income. It involved working with a program for teenagers in foster care. There was a lot of training and activities and many interactions with social workers from Family Services offices around the region. The assistantship was set up that I would train under the director of this program as his assistant for six months before I took over as the director. He was another graduate student who was finishing his degree. When I first started working with him, he told me that I would have to be patient as I worked with all the social workers from the various Family Services offices because they were not friendly people and were often irritable and hard to work with. I filed that in the back of my brain and moved forward, doing the best I could to learn the program so I could eventually take over as director when the time came.

Fast forward about one year. I had functioned as director for six months and really enjoyed my work. I made a lot of friends from all the Family Services offices with which I worked. One day, I paused and pondered about what the previous director had said about these workers. I wondered why he had told me they were often irritable and difficult to work with, because I enjoyed my relationships with them so much. I remembered that the previous director was kind of a negative and irritable person. It dawned on me what was really happening. This previous director had developed a certain type of relationship with Family Services personnel based on the kind of person he was. I was pretty upbeat and friendly with everyone and, consequently, I established fairly positive relationships with these workers and enjoyed my time with them.

What kind of world have you created for yourself? What kind of community, school, home, or workplace have you created? Are there things you can do differently that will, ultimately, change the world in which you find yourself? Remember, *you create your own world.*

You Gotta Deal With Difficult People

Years ago, a friend named Molly was in a grocery store with her little daughter. The store was crowded and shopping carts were moving in all directions. As Molly came to an intersection of two aisles, a woman approached from another direction. Molly responded out of reflex and hurriedly pushed her cart through the intersection. The other woman made a rude gesture to my friend. Molly was shocked and bothered by the behavior of this woman and also upset that her young daughter had witnessed this.

What would you do? How would you respond to this woman in a crowded grocery store who made a rude gesture to you? What would most people do? What if it was in a private, secluded place where no one else observed the behavior? Would you respond differently? What if it was on the road and you were driving a car?

125

Let's consider a spectrum of options that includes being passive, assertive, or aggressive.

The passive response would be to do nothing and just go about your business. Being passive can be an effective and appropriate response in many situations. However, there is a downside to being passive all the time. Some people take unfair advantage of you if you are seen as a doormat. Doormats get walked on, and if you don't want people to walk all over you, you may need to stand up for yourself and not tolerate certain behaviors from others, particularly if there is a pattern of behavior that continually demeans you. The upside to being passive is that you don't get pulled into a lot of drama and you can often avoid unnecessary conflict. There are a lot of immature people who do some pretty stupid things. If we had to respond to all of them we would waste a lot of time and energy.

The other end of the spectrum is being aggressive. The aggressive response can be harsh and excessive and could include verbal or physical hostility. The aggressive response is rarely a good option. It often escalates a situation and creates more problems. Our correctional facilities are full of people who chose aggression. Being aggressive can ruin relationships simply because most people don't like to be treated in hostile ways. There are some occasions, however, when an aggressive response may be appropriate. If an intruder breaks into my home and attempts to harm my family, I would aggressively protect them. In most settings where someone tries to physically harm you, an aggressive response is appropriate.

Now moving towards the middle. The assertive response is confident and direct but respectful. Assertive people do not ignore the issue or just let it go. They face it because it is worthy of being addressed. They are not afraid of speaking directly to people but, when they do, they maintain their composure and seek a resolution to the problem.

Now back to the grocery store with Molly. She did not respond at the moment the woman made the rude gesture, but she was concerned. She finished her shopping and proceeded to the checkout stands, and there was the woman. Moving from passive to assertive, she decided to address the issue. You may be surprised how she handled this tricky situation. Molly was assertive, but dealing with difficult people often requires us to swallow our pride to achieve the desired outcome, which is not to win but to resolve the conflict. She approached the woman and said, "Ma'am, I'm sorry if I did something to offend you. I did not mean to and I'm sorry."

What do you think of that response? Is it what you expected? Do you think Molly thought she did anything wrong? No, not for a second, but she sized up the situation beautifully. She wasn't sure what she was dealing with. This woman had already reacted in an aggressive way with virtually no provocation. My friend did not want to aggravate the situation but was doing whatever she could to improve it.

There is something else in play here that I call the *scoreboard principle*. Many people, in fact, all people at some time in their lives, have a scoreboard in their head and when someone says something derogatory or does something hurtful, they give the person a point, making the score 1 - 0. Since I am now behind in the score I need to retaliate to even the score. Sound familiar? Have you done this? Does this ever work? You know the answer. No, it doesn't work. It just fuels the fire and continues the conflict which, for some, can last a lifetime. How sad that is, but it is true.

Now, Molly is a sensible and mature woman who does not have a scoreboard in her head. She did not need to even the score because there was no score. Her only motive was to defuse the situation and resolve any conflict.

After Molly's response, the woman said to her, "No, I'm sorry. I overreacted. I'm having a bad day and nobody ever notices me." Wow! Did you expect that? That is truly what happened, the situation was defused and the conflict resolved. It can be difficult to attempt a resolution by swallowing our pride and truly desiring to defuse the conflict rather than win an argument, or worse, to beat the other person at her own game, but it usually is worth the effort.

To teach another principle, let's start with this experience but make it a little more challenging. Pretend that when Molly apologized the lady responded in a hostile way. "Yeah, you cut me off; you better watch where you're going." Whoa. How would you respond? Would you start keeping score and choose to be aggressive? "Lady, you are impossible. I tried to be nice but you just don't get it."

At this point, you realize that this woman really *doesn't get it* and is not going to be reasonable. It will do you no good to attempt to reason with her. She is convinced that her behavior is perfectly acceptable and justified, and that you are twisted in your thinking and behavior. The thing to do now is to simply walk away and not waste more time or effort trying to change a person who is not ready for a change. Many people become extremely frustrated when someone is not willing to change, so we continue to try to persuade or force them to change because *our way* is the *right way*. It never works. Remember, you can't force anyone to change, not even a two-year-old.

The greater question here is: Who are you and what kind of person do you choose to be? This is the overriding message of this book. Are you in control of you, in control of your thoughts, your moods, your actions, and, ultimately, the kind of person you are and want to become? Or is something outside of you in control and driving you to do things and be the person you are or are becoming? There are countless examples of people in history, even within your lifetime, who took the high road and, against great odds and persecution, chose to remain in control of what they think, do, and ultimately the kind of person they want to become. Mother Theresa, Nelson Mandela, and Gandhi are some of the more famous ones, but you know people today who are like this.

Ask yourself which is the better way of living, taking charge of what you think, feel, and do and the kind of person you are today and want to be in the future, or is it better to be tossed to and fro by forces outside yourself, over which you have little control, to determine the person you are today and who you will become? We often note the great moral character of others and mistakenly believe they have it easier than we do. They didn't have to deal with a coworker like this narcissistic, inconsiderate person we have to deal with every day. They didn't have a mother who is so difficult and challenging and anyone in my shoes would feel the same way and would snap.

Here's a 1957 quotation by Allen Saunders, paraphrased by John Lennon decades later, that is appropriate now: "Life is what happens to us while we are making other plans." The Bible says it well when Jesus asks us to love our enemies and to do good to them that hate us and persecute us. This way of allowing others to determine our mood, our behavior, how our day goes, and ultimately the kind of person we are is a much lower and immature level of functioning. That's how little children function at their level of social and moral development. You take my toy then I take your toy. You hit me and I hit you back. That's the old "eye for an eye and tooth for a tooth" philosophy. Remember the pinball person.

Now don't misunderstand. I'm not saying it's easy. We all take the low road at times, but we can become better at taking the high road. If we do this, we will begin to see the result in our improved moods and attitudes and the kind of person we see ourselves becoming. Do you enjoy being angry and irritable? Do

131

you like it when someone does something inconsiderate or down right mean and you let it ruin your day? Do you like being a pawn for others to control? I don't believe you do. I believe you can do better. Try it, you just might like it.

Section 5—Now, Make It Happen

Make Up Your Mind To Be Happy

Abundant Gratitude

Behavior Is The Best Medicine

It's Time

133

Make Up Your Mind To Be Happy

Happiness does not depend upon who you are or what you have. It depends solely upon what you think.

Dale Carnegie

Years ago in Peru, torrential rains over many days caused mudslides that wiped out several villages where residents lost everything. People gathered to help and to report on the devastation. One man noticed a native woman with her children around her and her husband working to salvage what they could of their belongings. She was smiling when this man approached and spoke to her. He wondered how, amid all the destruction and the loss of her home, she could smile and seem happy. She responded, "I have my children and my husband. We are all okay. Yes, we lost our home and most of our belongings but those things can be replaced. We have what really matters."

Was she just being brave or was she genuinely happy? Of course, this was a devastating, stressful experience, and she was not glad she lost her home and possessions. Nevertheless, her focus on what really matters and having gratitude for what she still had allowed her to be happy.

Now let's jump to Hollywood, the one in California. Think about celebrities you have seen in the news who have been divorced or in court or admitted to a rehab program. To most of the world, they seem to have everything. Millions of fans at one time or another wished they could trade places with any of those celebrities and then they would be truly happy. If we just had the money they had, or their looks, or their fame and popularity, then we would really be happy. The crazy thing is these celebrities had the money, the looks, and the popularity, but it didn't guarantee happiness. We have even seen some of these celebrities take their own lives. What happened? Perhaps Dale Carnegie was right; happiness depends on what we think.

When I was a college student, going to school full-time and recently married, I worked part-time to support myself and my new wife. My life was stressful. During this time I read *Man's Search For Meaning* by Victor Frankl. Frankl was a Jew from Austria during Hitler's reign of terror. Nazi soldiers invaded Austria and rounded up thousands of Jews, put them on boxcars, and shipped them to Auschwitz, the infamous Nazi concentration camp in Poland. He endured three horrific years and witnessed many of his fellow Jews be killed or die from the terrible conditions in the camp. When the war ended, those who remained in camp were liberated and Victor Frankl wrote about his experience.

I distinctly remember being so happy after reading this book. My life, which had not changed from my previously stressful life the week before I read the book, was the greatest life ever. Or did something change? Yes, something did change. Something had to change for me to be so happy and feel so good about my life. The change was in my *thinking*. I wasn't locked in a Nazi concentration camp with broth for meals, a wood slab for a bed, and the horror of wondering if I would be killed any day. I was free to walk outside my apartment, to walk down the street, to go to the store, to school, to work, or simply do whatever I wanted to do without the fear of death looming over me.

If happiness depends on what we think, and what we think is our choice, then *happiness is a choice*. As Dr. Frank Crane attributed to Abraham Lincoln in 1914,

"Most people are as happy as they make up their minds to be."

As a teenager, I remember looking forward to being my own person. I was sure that would make me happy. Then, much to my surprise, being away from my parents and on my own didn't make me happy. My focus shifted to the next phase of life. I wanted companionship and a family. I sought out a wife and eventually married a wonderful woman during my undergraduate years.

I was happy to find a lovely companion, but I still had stressors and felt pressure to finish school and take care of myself and my wife. We were extremely desirous to have children and raise a family. In fact, this didn't come easily for us and became a source of much pain and distress. We didn't care as much about job or money or other things: we wanted a child. With a little medical intervention, a miracle happened and we had a baby, then another before I graduated. I finished my education and was able to secure gainful employment, and we had two more children in the next few years.

For a short time, I felt that I had arrived. I was glad to have a growing family and a job but, again, I still had stressors. I felt the need to be successful in my profession as a psychologist.

As my life has continued to progress, I have learned that every phase of life has its challenges and nothing brings me happiness automatically.

Many people spend much of their life working hard trying to make as much money as they can. They use their hard-earned money to buy things, many things, like a big house, cars, boats, jewelry, nice clothes, and storage sheds to keep it all in. They mistakenly believe *things* will bring them happiness. I've never heard of a man or woman on their death bed say, "I wish I had worked harder so I could have bought more things." It is much more common to hear, "I wish I hadn't worked so much but had spent more time with my family and the ones I love."

As my wife and I face the empty nest phase of our lives, we are getting rid of many of the things we've accumulated and desire simply to be closer to our children and spend time with them.

In addition to material things, many people believe that to be happy the world needs to treat them kindly, do nice things for them, and be generous to them. Without this, they cannot and will not have happiness.

The trouble really hits when they believe that moving to a new neighborhood, or getting accepted to a certain school, or finding the right job, or finding the perfect spouse, or having a family will bring happiness into their life.

You have seen and know some of these people, and maybe you are one of them, always looking for the perfect neighborhood, school, job, boyfriend/girlfriend, spouse, to make them happy.

This is a miserable way to live. You can clearly see why, right? You're always searching for happiness but never finding it because you're looking outside yourself in people and places and things, when what you really need is to look inside yourself and change the way you perceive life and how you choose to interact with the world.

Abundant Gratitude

Gratitude is a close cousin to happiness. Gratitude is the act of appreciating what we have and not always seeking for something better. Not that we shouldn't try to improve ourselves and our circumstances, but we should appreciate the moment and what we have at the moment. You know the old saying, "you often don't appreciate something until it is gone."

Just like happiness, gratitude has everything to do with how you choose to think. As I work in the hospital with adolescents who struggle with depression and other emotional disorders, I like to bring pictures into our groups, and share stories of individuals who have been injured in military service or have lost limbs in accidents. Then we talk a little bit about their lives.

There is the story of Jessica Lynch, a young soldier who joined the army at age 18 so she could obtain the funds to pursue her education and become a teacher. Jessica was deployed to Iraq where her company was ambushed and she was taken captive as a Prisoner of

War (POW). Some of her comrades were killed in the ambush and she sustained significant injuries to her legs. The U. S. negotiated her release along with other POWs and Jessica was sent to Germany for medical care and eventually back to the U. S. to complete her rehab. She enrolled in college and completed her teaching degree and tells the story of walking across the stage to receive her diploma. "I'll walk across the stage on a leg that doesn't work well anymore," she said, "but at least it's attached. At least I have a leg. My friend was killed in the ambush. At least I'm alive." She was grateful for what she had and realized it could have been a lot worse.

I saw a story on television of another soldier who had been badly injured in an attack in Afghanistan. What caught my attention was the news anchor's statement, "A soldier receives double arm transplant." I knew you could transplant kidneys and hearts and corneas, but I had no idea you could transplant arms. This soldier lost not only both of his arms, he also lost his legs. In this brief news piece, it showed a 27-year-old man with his newly attached arms all bandaged up. He rolled his wheelchair into the room of reporters with his doctors accompanying but not assisting him in any way. He spoke freely with the reporters and said, while gesturing with his newly attached arms, "I could do without my legs but I really wanted my arms. You use your arms to express yourself." His attitude was amazing. The doctors noted that it would take months for his arms to become fully functional but that process was going to move along much quicker for this soldier because of his extremely positive attitude.

After sharing some of these stories with the adolescents in my group, I ask if anybody even thought about themselves *walking* into the group room that day. Of course, no one thought about it. They did it automatically and took their legs for granted. I then ask if anyone has ever been on crutches. Let me ask you that same question. Have you ever had to use crutches due to an ankle or knee injury? Many people have experienced this even for just a short time. Was it challenging? Did you miss being able to walk everywhere you go? Speaking for myself, I have been on crutches three different times. The last time was in my adult years and was the longest, two whole months. Yikes! What a hassle! Up and down stairs, trying to carry my clipboard, testing materials and paperwork in the hospital. My underarms were killing me and I developed some serious callouses on the palms of my hands. Was I ever glad to get off those darn crutches.

I ask if any of these adolescents have been homeless and if they have had to go days without food. Sadly, I usually have one or two in my group who admit to having had such an experience. Although their hospital beds are fairly basic and the food is not five-star gourmet cuisine, they begin to appreciate that they have shelter and food.

Just going out camping for a night or two for many of us who don't profess to be seasoned outdoorsman will build a greater appreciation for the modern conveniences we enjoy most days. Many of us probably have cursed our old, broken down cars and coveted our neighbor's fancy new car. When your car is in the shop, however, and you need to rely on another person to pick you up and transport you to and from work, you are pretty eager to get that old beater back because it fairly reliably took you to and from work in all kinds of weather for many years.

Another personal example I use has to do with my voice. As a boy I often came down with laryngitis that would last for a week or two. Some days I would stay home from school but most days I didn't really feel that bad, I just didn't have much of a voice, so I would go to school. How embarrassed I was when someone tried to talk to me or the teacher called on me. I hated it! When I finally got my voice back I was so happy I could just talk. It never failed, however, that after a couple of weeks of having my voice back it was just another day and I once again took my voice for granted. I try to remind myself every day of how fortunate I am to have a voice and that I can speak to people freely without embarrassment. I try to remind myself that my body functions quite well and I have legs and arms that work.

One day recently, driving to work, I was not excited about facing some of my young patients at the hospital. I felt sorry for myself and wished briefly that I could be in a different set of circumstances. Near my home I passed the street where a friend of mine lives. This friend recently was diagnosed with Stage 4 colon cancer and was given just a 10 percent chance of surviving. It hit me like a brick wall. My friend would probably give anything to be in my shoes, simply going to work, which he can no longer do because he is on disability so he can undergo intensive treatment in an attempt to save his life.

In 2003, two psychologists, Robert Emmons from the University of California at Davis and Michael McCollough of Southern Methodist University, published a paper on gratitude. Their paper was the result of three studies involving a few hundred people and addressed the impact of gratitude on well-being. They discussed specific effects that were manifest within groups of people who cultivated a thankful outlook on life. They found that individuals who were more grateful:

experienced heightened levels of joy and happiness;

were optimistic about the future;

felt better about their lives as a whole;

exercised more regularly;

were more likely to help others;

had more energy, enthusiasm, and focus;

made greater progress toward achieving important personal goals;

slept better and awoke feeling refreshed;

felt stronger during trying times;

enjoyed closer relationships;

dealt with stress better;

got sick less often.

That is quite an array of positive conditions to enjoy, just from being grateful.

145

The message is to count your blessings and stop taking so many things for granted. Look at what you have to be grateful for and stop looking at what you don't have. Lacking gratitude will only leave you wanting something more and never being fully satisfied.

Behavior Is The Best Medicine

All too often we look to medicine to take care of our problems. This is the medical model: I am sick so I go to the doctor to get medicine to make me better. This philosophy has carried over into mental health. I go to the doctor and share my emotional issue and she gives me medicine to help me get better. Don't misunderstand. I recognize the place pharmaceuticals have in society and in addressing various emotional disorders, but there are many things we can do to help ourselves besides taking a pill.

During the 20 plus years I have practiced as a psychologist, I have seen thousands of patients with thousands of symptom presentations. No matter what the presenting problem is, though, I always review with my patients what is called behavior medicine. This medicine is not in the form of a pill but rather it is *behavior*, things you can *do* to help yourself. Whether an individual presents with depression, anxiety, or anger issues, I always discuss these four components of behavior medicine.

147

The first component is **sleep**. Our body needs sufficient sleep to function well emotionally and physically, yet so many people neglect this fundamental need. The most common reason that people have difficulty sleeping is that they cannot turn their mind off, especially when stressed or anxious or just thinking too much about problems or what is coming the next day. Often, these thoughts are irrational and cause us unnecessary worry. We cannot make ourselves fall asleep, so we focus on bedtime routines that help us become more relaxed and condition us for sleep.

A key piece to the falling asleep puzzle is on the other end of sleep, the waking up part. While you cannot make yourself fall asleep, you can make yourself wake up. What often happens is people develop a pattern of difficulty falling asleep and end up tossing and turning until 2:00 am before finally crashing. They stay in bed until 10:00 am. They slowly shift their body clock such that it becomes harder and harder to get to sleep at a reasonable hour. When 10:00 pm rolls around, they are not tired because they slept until 10:00 am which leads to not being tired until 2:00 am again.

Hyrum Smith, former CEO of FranklinCovey, Co., gave wise advice on this subject. He talked about what he called "the magic three hours" which is 5:00-8:00

am. He spoke of getting his children up and exercising, reading from scriptures, doing chores, and eating a healthy breakfast. Someone in the audience was amazed at how he and his wife were able to get kids up at 5:00 am and asked what his secret was. "I make them go to bed at 9:00 pm," was his answer. Another hand shot up and asked, "How do you get kids to go to bed at 9:00 pm?" Mr. Smith responded very simply, "I make them get up at 5:00."

The second component of behavior medicine is **diet and nutrition**. What we put into our bodies is paramount and will greatly influence how we feel and function physically and emotionally. Everything in life seems geared for high speed. We want everything fast and easy, including our food. We are so busy and all too often fall into the bad habit of picking up fast food or settling for processed food that does little good by way of nourishing us with the natural minerals and vitamins our bodies need.

Taking time to plan healthy meals and snacks with fresh fruits and vegetables while avoiding high sugar content foods and processed foods help immensely with the way we feel physically, which ultimately ties into the way we feel emotionally.

We hear again and again that one-third of the population is considered obese. This leads to the third component of behavior medicine which is **exercise**. So often I hear patients say they don't have time to exercise or can't afford it. I say you cannot afford to *not* exercise. The time you spend exercising will be gained back in efficiency at work, more restful sleep, and more positive mood, which adds up to giving you more time to do things that are important and necessary.

Some people have physical ailments that limit exercise. The irony is they often wouldn't have these physical ailments if they had taken better care of their bodies and were more physically fit. Whatever shape you are in, it is good to start slowly and it would be wise to consult a medical doctor to determine what your body can and cannot do. Just about everyone can walk or do simple stretching at home. It need not cost money and the time it takes is minimal. Again, you will gain time in the long run in efficiency and decreased fatigue and sickness.

There are countless options like swimming, aerobics, cycling, weightlifting, or any number of things that will burn calories and increase cardiovascular fitness and muscle tone. Many smartphones have a pedometer function to keep track of your daily miles while walking around at work or grocery shopping or walking in your neighborhood or just walking around the house and up and down stairs. Instead of taking five minutes to find the perfect parking spot close to the main entrance of a store, park out at the edge of the lot and walk to the door. I work at a hospital with several units and offices spread over five floors. I never take the elevator but instead walk the stairs throughout the day which gives me a lot of exercise that the elevator riders are missing.

The fourth and final component of behavior medicine is what I call **pleasurable events**. You must have regular enjoyable and fulfilling activities that rejuvenate you or you will burn out and life will be drudgery. For one person it may be a couple of nights a week going to a park to bird-watch. For someone else, it may be going fishing for a few hours early Saturday morning. It could be one night a week getting together with friends and bowling or shooting pool. It could be any number of things that simply lift your spirits and help you enjoy yourself.

I encourage you to try new things, too. Often we feel we wouldn't enjoy a certain activity so we never try it, but if we actually tried it we may like it. I had this experience shortly after buying our first home. The front walkway had a strip of dirt along the side for some landscaping. My wife wanted flowers planted so I gave in and planted flowers, something a masculine, sports-minded guy like me would never enjoy, right? Wrong! I planted those flowers and watered them and watched them grow and to my great surprise, I loved it. It was the greatest thing being able to beautify our little home and having neighbors comment on how pretty the flowers were. I took great pride in those flowers and have continued to enjoy landscaping to help beautify my property.

No matter what the issue may be for you, try applying these four components of behavior medicine in your life and see how much more physically and emotionally fulfilled you become.

It's Time

Time is a fascinating thing. We want more of it when we have not completed things we want to do, but we can't wait until it passes to bring us to some anticipated event. Probably there is no other time when we wish we had done things differently with our time than when facing the end of our mortal life. Ultimately, we all have the same amount of time every single day yet some people seem to do so much more with their time than others.

I learned an important principle about *time* a few years ago while meeting with a couple with marital struggles. At the end of a session, I suggested that the husband talk with his father who lived out of state. I thought it would help him to get input from his dad. When we met a week later, I asked about his conversation with his father. The man said he did not call his father as instructed because he *didn't have time.*

He didn't have time? I remember being perturbed by his remark. Never before did the question of time or not having time hit me so keenly. I found myself thinking, "You're kidding me. You didn't have time? You couldn't take 10 minutes to call your dad? You had just as much time as anyone else had this past week."

Now here's the principle about time. The issue wasn't that he didn't have time. The issue was that he *chose to do something else* with his time. If his wife had been hospitalized unexpectedly and he was home tending his three little children, and he chose to spend his time taking care of them instead of calling his father, that's understandable, but that's not what he said. When we say we didn't have time, that is totally false and inaccurate. It's like saying the time fairy snuck into your house and stole some of your time so you couldn't get the things done that you wanted to do. It's laughable, isn't it? The issue with time then becomes priorities and choices, because we all have 24 hours a day, no more, no less. What we choose to do with our time is totally up to us.

We all have a variety of time-consuming activities that do not produce anything of value. Let's do a little math to illustrate how quickly little chunks of time add up to constitute a significant block of time. How much time do you spend on social media each day? How much time do you spend watching TV? How much time on the computer surfing the net or playing games?

Let's say you spend two hours on social media and two hours watching a couple of TV shows every day. That's 4 hours. Out of 24 hours, you have 8 hours for sleep, which leaves you with 16 waking hours. So 4 hours is one fourth of your 16 waking hours, right? I like to frame it this way for a more powerful effect. How many months is one fourth of a year? That's 3 months, right? So we could say that when the year begins we are going to take January, February, and March and simply throw them away because we are spending that amount of time every year on social media and watching TV, relatively mindless activities that produce little of value in the long run. Wow, that looks different than a few hours a day, doesn't it? You can see how quickly time adds up.

This simple math works for better or for worse. Let's look at a way you could use time to your advantage by utilizing a little time every day to do something of lasting value. Let's take reading. Out of those 4 hours of social media/TV watching, we'll take just 1 hour. How many pages an hour can you read? Let's be fairly conservative and say 40 pages an hour. How many pages are in a typical book? For the sake of this illustration, let's use 400 pages for a typical book. If you read for one hour or 40 pages a day, you could read a whole book in just 10 days. Over the course of a year, you would read 36 books. You could read many of the classics in just one year and become that well-read person you've longed to be.

Let's look at two well-known books that many people read, the *Holy Bible* and the *Harry Potter* series. The Old and New Testaments combined in the King James Version total 1,590 pages. Reading for an hour, 40 pages per day, would enable you to finish the Old and New Testaments in just 40 days, or nine times in a year. You could read all 3,407 pages of the *Harry Potter* books in just 85 days, reading for an hour, 40 pages per day. You could read this book 90 times in a year. Ha ha.

Seriously, though, imagine how much better you would be at your job if you read the key literature in your field every year. That's how quickly time adds up and can be used to accomplish good things instead of wasting it away.

Planning is an important part of time management. If I don't plan my day when I'm not at work for 8-10 hours, time often slips away into many useless activities. Sometimes we think, "I don't have time to plan." Ah ha! Got you! What you mean is that you chose to do something else. If you don't take the time to plan, you are going to lose time and be much less effective. It doesn't have to be an elaborate, drawn out planning session. It can just take five minutes and involve simply identifying priorities and blocking off time chunks to devote to certain activities. Don't forget to plan leisure time. Sometimes we think if we plan we will simply be doing work or chores the whole time and have no fun. Plan some fun things to do. Plan some time just to relax.

Now don't misunderstand me. I'm not saying it's never true that you don't have enough time to do things. There are only 24 hours in a day, after all, so you will not have time to accomplish all the things you want. That's just a part of life. The issue is not needing to magically find another hour or two in the day but rather the number of things you are trying to pack into the time you have. This is a time management issue.

I remember a college student who came to see me with symptoms of anxiety and depression. I learned that she was trying to graduate after two more semesters so she could begin graduate school the next year. She was taking 18 credit hours a semester while working full-time. In my college career, I never took more than 16 hours a semester and only 12 hours a semester when I worked 20 hours a week. No wonder she was anxious and depressed. She had given herself a nearly impossible task and was beating herself up because she was not superwoman. I told her she needed to decide what takes priority and adjust her schedule accordingly.

In many cases, we need to say no to things that are a lesser priority. If you continue to have a problem with this, you may need to explore some of your personal paradigms. It may relate to a completely different issue of feeling inadequate unless we are doing and, theoretically, accomplishing an endless amount of things.

Again, we all have the same amount of time each day. Time will work against you if left unmanaged, but with a little effort it can be made to work for you in predictable and fantastic ways, depending only on how you choose to organize yourself.

Just like anything else, time management is a skill and the more we practice it the better we will become at it. It's not rocket science. You can do this. You just have to devote a little *time* to it.

And Finally....

Life can be quite complicated when we consider the complexity of the issues we each face, but the foundational principles about who we are and how we choose to interact with the world are fairly simple.

The plague of teen suicide has been in the forefront of my mind lately as a young man who attended high school with my daughter and who is the son of a coworker committed suicide. I can hardly stand the thought of another child taking his life because he feels he is not a good person and there is no future for him. What ultimately drives people to contemplate and eventually commit suicide is based on perceptions that are irrational. If someone thinks they are worthless, that construct doesn't exist anywhere but in their own mind. If someone thinks there is no future for them, again, this is not true but is a perception that exists nowhere else in the world but in their mind.

I hope after reading this book you have been educated, to a small degree, on some basic principles for

159

managing your life. My desire is for you to be empowered to the extent that you truly change the world in which you live by seeing it, and the people in it, differently. Having this new perspective, you can now choose to interact with your world in a very different manner that will bring much greater autonomy and happiness.

I always tell my patients I want them to get into cognitive shape. Similar to being in good physical shape, good cognitive shape takes consistent effort over time. Review the chapters of this book often. Use them as guides to healthy and happy living by applying the principles discussed. Don't let another day go by living in the same old world you have been living in for years. Do something, small or big, that will demonstrate you have indeed changed because you read this book, which is the ultimate design in my writing.

I hope that makes you happy.

About The Author

To know what makes people tick. That was the desire of Brian Chandler as a boy growing up in a suburb of Boston, where he developed a fascination with human behavior. On subways and buses around town, he found himself observing the diversity and complexity of the human organism.

This bred within him a yearning to better understand the hearts and minds of men and women throughout the world. A psychology class at Medford High School piqued his interest and led him to study Psychology at Brigham Young University (BYU) in Provo, Utah.

Early in his studies, he took a two-year hiatus to serve as a missionary in Taiwan, where he learned to speak Mandarin Chinese and came to see the world from a whole new perspective while living among the Chinese people and learning their culture.

Chandler returned to BYU to complete his Bachelor's Degree in Psychology. He met and married his beautiful wife, Susan, also a student at BYU. After graduation, they moved to Manhattan, Kansas. Chandler attended graduate school at Kansas State University and completed a Master's Degree in Marriage and Family Therapy.

The time at Kansas State was enlightening and helped Chandler understand the powerful impact of interpersonal relationships and how they influence thought and emotion. In his desire to pursue a degree that would have a strong applied clinical focus, he completed his Doctoral Degree at Indiana University of Pennsylvania where he studied Clinical Psychology.

While in Pennsylvania, two children were born to the Chandler family—a son and a daughter. After three years, the family moved back to Utah so that Chandler could complete a Pre-Doctoral Internship at BYU's Counseling and Development Center and a Post-Doctoral Residency with Assessment and

Psychotherapy Associates in Salt Lake City. Both of these training experiences helped shape his passion for cognitive behavior therapy and understanding the power of the human mind.

Eager to apply all of his learning about human behavior, Dr. Chandler moved his family to Springfield, Missouri, where he accepted a job as a staff psychologist at Burrell Behavioral Health, the mental health division of Cox Hospital.

Two more daughters were added to the growing Chandler family early in their time in Springfield, adding to his opportunity to learn first-hand about human development, behavior, and relationships. After two years, Dr. Chandler joined a group of psychologists in private practice and spent a significant amount of time at Lakeland Regional Hospital, a psychiatric hospital in Springfield that primarily treats children and adolescents.

The past 20 years were dedicated to evaluating and treating a range of individuals of all ages, cultures, and socioeconomic backgrounds. Dr. Chandler has learned that although there are unique qualities, attributes, and challenges with each of us, the fundamental principles surrounding our emotional well-being are the same.

People choose their thoughts that create files in their brain that drive how they feel and ultimately how they choose to behave. Knowing that we can be active participants in the happiness we experience through managing our thoughts effectively is a wonderful thing that Dr. Chandler wants the whole world to understand, especially you.

Tell Me What You Think

If you found this book useful or otherwise enjoyable, tell your family, friends, and coworkers. Please follow this link to leave a review on Amazon. I will read and consider what you say because I want to provide the best books I can. Your input helps.

> Use this link to review *Approaching Life With Confidence: Defeat Depression and Anxiety by Taking Charge of Your Mind*:
>
> http://amzn.to/2yr0lWe

Thanks so much for your support.

Follow Dr. Chandler at *mypracticalpsychologist.com*.

49369617R00098

Made in the USA
Middletown, DE
16 October 2017